Liberation Theology

Also by Robert McAfee Brown

The Bible Speaks to You

Making Peace in the Global Village

Persuade Us to Rejoice:
The Liberating Power of Fiction

Religion and Violence—Second Edition,
With a New Introduction by the Author

Saying Yes and Saying No:
On Rendering to God and Caesar

The Significance of the Church

Spirituality and Liberation:
Overcoming the Great Fallacy

Theology in a New Key:
Responding to Liberation Themes

Unexpected News:
Reading the Bible with Third World Eyes

Liberation Theology
An Introductory Guide

Robert McAfee Brown

Westminster/John Knox Press
Louisville, Kentucky

Unless otherwise noted, scripture quotations are taken from *The Revised English Bible*, © Oxford University Press and Cambridge University Press, 1989. Used by permission.

Scripture quotations marked KJV are from the King James Version of the Bible.

Book design by Drew Stevens

First edition

Published by Westminster/John Knox Press
Louisville, Kentucky

This book is printed on recycled acid-free paper that meets the American National Standards Institute Z39.48 standard. ∞

PRINTED IN THE UNITED STATES OF AMERICA
9 8 7 6 5 4 3 2

Library of Congress Cataloging-in-Publication Data

Brown, Robert McAfee, 1920–
    Liberation theology : an introductory guide / Robert McAfee Brown. — 1st ed.
            p.   cm.
    Includes bibliographical references.
    ISBN 0-664-25424-1 (pbk. : acid-free)

    1. Liberation theology.   I. Title.
BT83.57.B764 1993
230'.046—dc20   92-30934

To the Children
of
Zácomil
and
Ocotal

Contents

Author's Note   ix
Acknowledgments   xiii
Introduction: Situating Ourselves   1

1

A New Way of Understanding People   19

(the human side of God's story)

> Making Connections
> The Human Story and God's Story
> Four Recurring Themes

2

A New Way of Seeing the World   35

(1492 and all that)

> Different Ways of Using the Past
> Learning from Las Casas
> A New Starting Point—
>   And Three Follow-ups

3

A New Way of Encountering God   51

("to know God is to do justice")

> Theology as a Love Letter
> Theology as the "Second Act"
> Critical Reflection on Praxis
>   in the Light of the Word of God
> The Good News of Liberation
> Jesus as Liberator
> To Know God Is to Do Justice

4

A New Way of Being the Church   69

(the genie that won't go back in the bottle)

The Discovery of the Future—
A Look at the Past
The Discovery of One Another—
The Base Communities
The Discovery of the Bible—
A Charter for Change
The Discovery of Conflict—
A Look at the Structures

5

Can There Be a New Way for Us? (1)   89

(liberation theology and North America)

Stop . . .
. . . Look . . .
. . . and Listen
It's *Kairos* Time . . .

6

Can There Be a New Way for Us? (2)   107

(our own liberation theology)

Is It *Kairos* Time for Us?
Three Cautions
Some Next Steps
A Concluding Biblical Image:
Servants in Pharaoh's Court

Study Questions   129

Notes and Resources   133

Author's Note

This book originated as a series of lectures for lay people at the Chautauqua Institution, Chautauqua, New York, during the week of August 19–23, 1991—a week dedicated to the study of present-day Latin America. My assignment was the role of the church in Latin America, and I concentrated on the emergence of liberation theology and its meaning for North America.

I stress this context lest the impression be given that liberation theology is an exclusively Latin American reality. Nothing could be further from the truth; liberation theology exists wherever there is oppression, and there are few parts of the globe, as a consequence, where movements for liberation are not this very day growing in size and intensity—South Africa, the Philippines, Sri Lanka, Singapore, China, Pacific rim nations, India, not to mention articulations of liberation theology within our own shores by African Americans, feminists and womanists, Hispanics, gays and lesbians, and many others.

In this rich context, Latin America can be accorded pride of place only as *one example* or case study of the widespread concern of oppressed people to take control of their destinies, in order to live decent, free, and fulfilled lives. In a somewhat similar fashion, I have dealt chiefly with Roman Catholic expressions of liberation theology. This does not mean that Protestant expressions are unimportant (an impression that I, as a Protestant, would not want to give) but simply that within a limited space not everything could be said.

Some readers may feel misgivings about my ongoing

critique of our nation's political and economic policies as
they relate to poor and oppressed peoples. Here I must
simply state my conviction that much of the injustice in
the world today must be laid at our own doorstep. I do not
consider it "patriotic" to gloss over this fact. On the
contrary, I am persuaded that true patriots are always
those who try to call their country from what it descriptively *is* to what it ideally *ought to be*. I am firmly committed to the great American ideal of "liberty and justice for
all," and because of that commitment feel obligated to
point out places where the actuality is "liberty and justice
for *some*."

I am going to assume that this is a proposition self-
evident enough not to need extensive defense throughout
the text.

Although I have done sufficient editing to make the
book reflect the written rather than the spoken word, I
have tried to keep the informal atmosphere of the original
presentations, and to write in such a way that previous
acquaintance with the subject matter is not demanded.
The chapters will have failed if they are not informative
and clear on their own terms. For those, however, who
wish to pursue certain matters in more detail, I have
provided references and bibliographical suggestions in
the Notes.

Special thanks to Ross and Flora McKenzie of the Department of Religion of the Chautauqua Institution, who
not only arranged for my visit but were a wonderful host
and hostess as well. Similar thanks to an audience that
provided stimulating questions and discussion after each
lecture, frequently pushing me to revise my initial draft
before it appeared in the unforgiving finality of a pub-

lished text, and to Jack Nelson-Pallmeyer, not only for insights over the years but for help at the eleventh hour.

Each afternoon that I lectured, the Rev. Dr. Gustavo Parajon (Baptist minister, medical doctor, and head of CEPAD, the evangelical development organization in Nicaragua) was preaching in the morning. As I said frequently during my own presentations, and wish to repeat here, after hearing him each morning I could not fail to note (sometimes to my discomfort) the contrast between my second-hand reports, and his first-hand example— one who has been living out of the liberating power of the Christian faith through a lifetime of service in his native Nicaragua, a country wracked by a ten-year civil war that my government sponsored and financed. His ability to think, share, challenge—and forgive—make my efforts at communication seem paltry by comparison. I am indebted to him and his wife, Joan, who has carried on her own share of liberation activities, for showing us all at first hand the power of a commitment to God that spells itself out in selfless dedication to God's children.

R.M.B.

Lent 1992

Acknowledgments

Grateful acknowledgment is made for permission to reprint the following copyrighted material:

Altered versions of articles by Robert McAfee Brown that appeared in *Christianity and Crisis* are reprinted with permission. Copyright Christianity and Crisis, 537 W. 121st St., New York, NY 10027. One year subscription (19 issues), $24.00.

Altered versions of articles by Robert McAfee Brown that appeared in *Commonweal* are reprinted with permission of the journal.

The table on pp. 138–139 is reprinted from Robert McAfee Brown, *Gustavo Gutiérrez: An Introduction to Liberation Theology* (Maryknoll, N.Y.: Orbis Books, 1990), and is used by permission of Orbis Books.

Excerpt from "Manifesto: The Mad Farmer's Liberation Front" in *The Country of Marriage,* copyright © 1973 by Wendell Berry, reprinted by permission of Harcourt Brace Jovanovich, Inc.

Excerpts from *The Road to Damascus: Kairos and Conversion* are reprinted by permission of The Center of Concern, 3700 13th St. N.E., Washington, DC 20017.

Introduction: Situating Ourselves

One of Alan Paton's novels is titled *Ah, But Your Land Is Beautiful*. It is a common phrase on the lips of visitors to South Africa, their instinctive response to the land's natural beauty—a beauty that provides an ironic backdrop for the ugliness still imposed on it by human beings.

Riding from Rio Blanco to Paiwas, in central Nicaragua, evokes Paton's title for me.[1] The sheer beauty of the sharply etched mountain ranges, the vigor of the rivers and streams, the pastures that furnish provender for sleek Cebu cattle, the graceful lines of the tiny thatched-roof houses, bring to mind another phrase from Paton as well, the opening lines of *Cry, the Beloved Country*, which, transposed into the Nicaraguan setting, read: "There is a lovely road that runs from Rio Blanco into Paiwas. These hills are grass-covered and rolling, and they are lovely beyond any singing of it."

Beauty and loveliness do, indeed, abound in Nicaragua, but so do anxiety and terror, even though "the war" has technically ended. For this is no paradise or Eden. It is a fallen world, ravaged by the ugliness of a war that lasted a decade, as contra soldiers, financed by the U.S. government, used the mountain ranges as bases for guerrilla raids, ambushed trucks as they slowed down to ford streams, burned crops, killed cattle, and demolished the graceful houses of the *campesinos*.

My friend Trinidad lives with his parents and seven brothers and sisters in a one-room house in the *Cooperativa de los Héroes y Martires de Rio Negro*—a name chosen to commemorate those who fell defending their families from a contra attack at the nearby river. The cooperative is a long, twisty, bumpy hour north of Boaco in Nicaragua. Not a beautiful road this time, but an essential lifeline for the members of the cooperative. Five miles farther down the road are the charred remains of another cooperative the contras gutted with fire bombs. Some of Trinidad's friends reside permanently beneath thirteen crosses half a mile in the opposite direction, site of a surprise attack by a contra group two hundred strong.

Maybe it's stretching things to call Trinidad my "friend." But at least he was my teacher, responding to the plea of the white-haired *gringo* who wanted to learn some rudimentary Spanish while living with Trinidad's family. His threefold pedagogical scheme was simplicity itself: I pointed, he named, I repeated: *la casa, el pollo, la escuela, el niño, la madre, la clínica.* At the end we pointed to each other: *los compañeros,* companions. A pretty deep level of communication: I'll claim him as a friend.

But he's there, and I'm back here. He is always in jeopardy, and I am almost always safe. Maybe the contras got him after my visit, which took place when the war was still going full tilt, the war my government initiated and sponsored. If the contras didn't get him, maybe starvation did, for the economy of Nicaragua has been in a shambles for years, not only during the war but even more after its ostensible finish; malnutrition and outright starvation are commonplace. Whatever has happened, the truth is that, short of a miracle, it's a low life expectancy for Trinidad and his friends—the legacy of the policies of my own government.

Trinidad, I wonder if you would still call me *compañero*, if you knew what I know . . .

It is the hands of Damos Echeverría that I will remember longest. As the guest of his family in the tiny Nicaraguan town of Paiwas, I saw his hands do all the ordinary things that human hands do: welcome strangers, caress children, sling hammocks (so that his guests would not have to sleep on the dirt floor with the lizards), and, with exquisite precision, scoop up rice and beans in the folds of a tortilla.

I also saw his hands do two other things, and the difference between them continues to haunt me.

At about eleven o'clock on Saturday night, there was a knock at the door, followed by a muffled conversation. A couple of minutes later Damos Echeverría went out into the darkness, hands clutching a rifle. Contra troops had been reported in the area, and Damos, along with other local militia members, had to defend the town against possible attack. We were, after all, in the middle of a war zone. So the hands of Damos Echeverría were ready to pull the trigger on that rifle and inflict death if necessary, so that his seven children might continue living.

The next morning during mass at the Paiwas parish Church of Christ the King, I saw those same hands sign the cross on the foreheads of children, and then—as the parish's minister of baptism—Damos Echeverría used his hands to pour water on their heads, administering the sacrament of baptism, a sign of the bestowal of new life in the midst of a world of death. I could not help reflecting that if my government had not been funding the contras, Damos Echeverría would not have had to train his hands to destroy life, but could have devoted them exclusively to the bestowing of new life.

Carmen Mendieta, Damos's wife, was the mother of those seven children, aged two to fifteen. Carmen was head of the local chapter of AMNLAE, the national Nicaraguan women's organization. She and Damos, a teacher of carpentry in the local school, were both Delegates of the Word, Catholic lay people who had been trained to work with children, help parents understand the meaning of baptism, instruct engaged couples in the meaning of marriage. Carmen, we realized in retrospect, got up earlier than usual each morning while we were there to prepare a more substantial breakfast for the two *gringos* staying with her than her own children would receive. Len Celabrese and I played with her seven children despite language difficulties, discovering that balloons are almost as good as a dictionary in breaking down language barriers.

A year after our visit, on the morning of December 2, 1987, Carmen Mendieta climbed into the back of a flatbed truck to go to Rio Blanco, fifteen miles away, to purchase electrical wire for the child-care center then under construction. On the way, the truck hit a Claymore mine, after which the contras sent a grenade through the windshield of the immobilized vehicle with enough force to kill Carmen and two other women sitting with her in the back of the truck.

Having made that same trip from Paiwas to Rio Blanco in that same truck one year earlier, I can imagine the place where the slaughter occurred—perhaps just past the beautiful turn in the road before fording the second creek at hubcap depth. I can imagine Carmen sharing her excitement about the child-care center with the woman and girl they had picked up on the way, I can imagine her saying that her daughter Jamalita, who wants to become a doctor, was going to work at the center with her. What I cannot imagine is why the Reagan administration viewed Carmen Mendieta as a sufficient threat to United States security to hire mercenaries to kill her.

And I now have to imagine something I never wanted to imagine. I have to imagine the hands of Damos Echeverría in the woodshop of the village school doing yet another thing—measuring boards, sawing them, planing them, nailing them together to fashion a coffin for the misshapen flesh that earlier that same day had been his wife and the mother of his children. I have to imagine those same hands shoveling out a shallow pit for his wife's grave, and covering the coffin with earth when Fr. Jaime has completed the service of burial. And I have to imagine those same hands holding his seven children close to him at the graveside as a light goes out in their lives forever.

The van driver who took us from the airport in Guatemala City for a meeting with Salvadoran Lutheran bishop-in-exile Medardo Gomez was affable, stocky, and informative. After helping us hoist our gear on top of the van, he drove efficiently through the evening traffic, pointing out items of interest. When we arrived at our destination, the site of the Norwegian Lutheran Church's activity in Guatemala, he helped us get our luggage off the van and into the conference room.

Our English-speaking leader asked us to identify ourselves to the Central Americans hosting us. We were three Lutheran bishops, an Anglican bishop, a Jesuit, and a small assortment of Catholics and Protestants. After we had made the rounds, I asked, in a fit of democratic zeal, if we could not learn the name of the van driver who had served us so well. With a smile, the van driver replied, "My name is Medardo Gomez."

As a Presbyterian, my experience with bishops has been limited. I had always supposed that other people drove bishops to meetings, rather than, as in this case, the reverse. If that is what bishops are really like, I have to revise my ecclesiology.

The reason Bishop Gomez was in Guatemala instead of his native El Salvador was that in El Salvador he had been imprisoned, tortured, and subjected to death threats too numerous to itemize. After his church was bombed, his offices raided and ransacked, and his family forced to leave the country because of death threats, Catholic and Protestant friends persuaded Bishop Gomez to leave the country as well.

The reason the rest of us were in Guatemala was that we had agreed to "accompany" him back to San Salvador so he could be with his people for the Feast of the Epiphany, arguably the biggest day in the life of Central American churches. Our presence was based on the consoling assumption that however much the Salvadoran authorities may hate *gringos,* and especially clerical *gringos,* they realize that it is bad PR to shoot them . . . or those in their company.

I will not deny that being the constant companion of a man threatened with violent death creates a certain tension within one. But there was an event at the San Salvador airport the next day that changed all that. When we entered the lobby after clearing customs, a huge crowd of Salvadorans awaited their bishop. (I had not realized there were that many Lutherans in all Central America.)

Beautiful reunions ensued as Medardo (nobody calls him "Bishop") embraced children and was embraced by old men, young men, old women, young women—embraces that included the rest of us, who were welcomed with genuine affection for having helped return their bishop to them. As I walked alongside Medardo, having been very conscious of worst-case scenarios, I suddenly realized—quite consciously—"I'm not afraid anymore." It was true. And then I realized—just as consciously—that the sudden departure of fear was not because I had suddenly become "brave," but simply because the courage and love of those committed folk had rubbed off on me, contagious beyond anything I could have imagined. We were sharing a great burden and a great joy together, which is what the communion of saints is all about.

By the end of our visit, I had learned two further things. First, I had learned why a Lutheran bishop is a threat to the government of El Salvador. The "sins" of Bishop Gomez are the sins of a host of others as well: he believes that the church's mission includes political involvement; that the gospel has a special concern for the poor that must be translated into the actions and policies of a nation; that a negotiated peace is preferable to an ongoing war; and that bishops often have to speak out and act in ways that are critical of the government. Such actions, whether by bishops or not, are actions punishable by death, and there are seventy-five thousand dead Salvadorans to attest to the accuracy of that proposition.

Second, I had learned why Bishop Gomez is so loved. Once he was back with his people, he realized that he could not truly be their bishop from the safety of another country, but must be in their midst, working, suffering, threatened, just like everybody else. And so Bishop

Gomez decided to return to El Salvador, not just for this visit on a feast day, but for the long haul. As these words are written, he and his family are still alive and working, but even with the precarious "peace" that has since come, one needs to check out the ongoing truth of that statement every few days.

At an ecumenical service on Epiphany, a Baptist pastor said to Bishop Gomez, "We Baptists don't have bishops. But you, Medardo, are our bishop."

Ditto for this Presbyterian.

Important things happen at other airports, too. My wife and I had been to Peru and Chile and were now leaving the Argentinian airport in Buenos Aires. In each country we had met with people visible in the life of the church, and also with people who, as the saying goes, "had to maintain a low profile." The rule about maintaining a low profile reads: "Stay out of sight so you won't get shot."

Before leaving the United States we had been given letters to transmit to some of the low-profile folk, who didn't need mail postmarked "USA" if their low profile was to remain effective. We were to mail the remaining letters when we got to Costa Rica. I remember one name on one of the envelopes was "Ignacio Ellacuria," someone whose profile later became very high, as we shall see. On the way to the airport we placed the letters in a large brown envelope, and buried it deep within a carryon suitcase. We had decided not to put them in the pieces of checked luggage, since they might be opened without our knowledge.

We made it through customs without incident, breathing appropriate sighs of relief. But the relief was premature. Tonight there was one more checkpoint than usual. Relief turned to surprise.

At the new checkpoint, the suitcase was opened, searched, and the large brown envelope extracted. Surprise turned to fear.

The large brown envelope was opened, and the letters taken out. Fear turned to terror.

What is there to feel beyond terror? If the letters were opened and their contents read, my friends would be dead and I would have betrayed them.

After a moment the inspector shrugged, put the letters back in the large brown envelope, returned the large brown envelope to the suitcase, and handed the suitcase to me, making what appeared to me at the time the most infinitely beautiful of all human gestures—an upraised thumb—meaning "Okay. No problem." He had been looking for drugs.

I rejoined my wife, whose pounding heart during this brief interminable episode had been reverberating in perfect timing with mine, audible, we were sure, to the farthest reaches of the airport complex. "Jesus Christ!" I breathed to her as I sat down. I'm still not sure whether it was a prayer or a curse.

But I *am* sure that for twenty-four seconds, close on to midnight, we both experienced the terror with which our sisters and brothers in Latin America have lived for years, during the twenty-four hours of every single day and every single night, when a knock at the door or an examination of one's belongings may mean death.

I have recently stood on holy ground. Two days ago, as I write this, I was on the spot in the University of Central America in San Salvador where six Jesuits, including Ignacio Ellacuria, their housekeeper, and her daughter, were murdered by units of the Salvadoran military.

I have been to shrines and sites of martyrdoms before, but never at a place where the results of human destruction were so palpably present: shattered glass all over the floors, walls pockmarked with hundreds of bullets, the roof buckled from heavy military bombardment, bloodstains still visible on the walls and floor and even on the ground outside where some of the killings had taken place.

Three days earlier I had spent an evening in the United States with Jon Sobrino, the only one of the Jesuits residing there who was *not* murdered, simply because he happened to be out of the country when the killings took place. I found I had a very strong need to enter his room, to experience where he would have been had he been home that fateful night. I was told that the body of one of the Jesuits who was killed outside had been brought back into Jon's room. As the killers were moving the body, they dislodged one of the books in the bookcase, which fell to the floor and was saturated with the martyr's blood. In the morning it was discovered that the book was Jürgen Moltmann's *The Crucified God*.

That symbolism still overpowers me. Yes, in Jesus of Nazareth, God too was "crucified," living out the fullness of human reality right up to the very nailprints. That we know by observation. But we also know, by faith, that the "crucified God" is also the "resurrected God." Which says at least that just as the crucified God was with the Jesuits in their death, so the Jesuits are with the resurrected God in their rising from the dead. That is the light of faith that sustains in time of darkness, when faith is tested to the uttermost.

Part of that "resurrection" is already visible, for the actions of the military, designed to scare off friends of the murdered Jesuits, did not work. There had been a ghastly appropriateness about the fact that all the priests were shot in the head, for the priests were thinkers, professors, researchers. They wrote. They spoke. And part of their message was that El Salvador need not remain a fear-ridden totalitarian state. And that constituted criticism of a government that would brook no criticism. But within days of the murders, hundreds of Jesuits all over the world were volunteering to take the places of the six martyrs. That is the beginning of a resurrection.

The response to the killings was supposed to be, "They've killed the Jesuits for speaking out, therefore we'd better not speak out or we will be killed also," but the actual result of the killings was, "They've killed the Jesuits for speaking out, therefore we must speak out for them."

At a memorial service for the slain, only a few hundred yards from the site of the killings, the most important comment was made by a young Salvadoran woman, who quite possibly did not know how to read or write, but certainly knew how to love: "Do not mourn their deaths," she counseled us, "imitate their lives."

The two brothers, Fernando and Ernesto Cardenal, are priests. Coming from a well-to-do background, they were driven to identify totally with the poor. But for siding with the revolutionary forces in their native Nicaragua, they have had their priestly "faculties" removed by Rome— they cannot celebrate mass, hear confession, or partici- pate as priests in other rites and sacraments of the church.

Fernando, a Jesuit, is tall, decisive, and brilliant. He

was minister of education all through the war years and headed the literacy program the Sandinista Party inaugurated when it came to power. He realized that in the war the odds were overwhelming that the contras, backed by Uncle Sam, would win. But, referring often to the biblical image of David and Goliath, he refused to believe that the outcome was preordained in Goliath's favor.

"What does the revolution mean?" we asked him. He told us about a taxi driver who said, "The revolution taught me and my son to read. Now my son is at the university." That is what the revolution means.

"How can a Christian like you work with Marxists?" we asked. He felt that the question was academic. "What counts is what is accomplished. 'By their fruits,' " he insisted, quoting a higher authority than Marx, " 'you shall know them,' not by their ideologies."

His brother Ernesto is a poet, minister of culture during the revolution, taking art *to* the people and eliciting art *from* the people. How does one describe a poet save by poetry?

To Ernesto: Poet/Revolutionary

We all need
times of beauty
moments of refreshment
by which to be empowered
for the struggle

But if we seek empowerment
exclusively
in havens of retreat
we soon begin to think

that beauty finds it dwelling place
apart from where the people are

You have shown us
that beauty also dwells
in misery's environs
and by its presence there
can work huge transformations

You have shown us
that there is nothing more beautiful
than a human face
on fire with the love of justice

Because for you there is no line
dividing art and revolution
your poems in themselves
are revolutionary acts
and revolution is empowered
by your verse

So
our friend
keep writing and keep doing
the rest of us will always need reminding
that Word and deed are one

The old man, who helped the three of us out of the van
in front of the El Cristo Salvador parish church in the
Zácomil area of San Salvador, was clearly the caretaker.
But when Ron Hennessey, the parish priest on loan from
Maryknoll, introduced him, it was not as the caretaker but
as the father of Octavio Ortíz, who had grown up in the

parish and was one of the first priest-martyrs of El Salvador. When we later went forward to receive Holy Communion, it was the father of Octavio Ortíz who gave us the bread of life.

When the fighting in the civil war actually entered the capital city, the parish church of Zácomil was a natural target, its members known for "forward-looking" concerns about poverty and children and peace and justice, nurtured by their exposure to such forward-looking folk as Amos, Jeremiah, and Jesús de Nazarét. So the military burst into the church, looted the office, stole the equipment, burned the files, spilled the reserved sacrament on the floor, and riddled the portrait of Octavio Ortíz, hanging on the rear wall, with bullet holes, as if in fear that he, though dead, might rise from the dead if they did not destroy him a second time. Boxes of munitions were brought in, photographed beside the altar, and then removed. (The pictures would be offered in court to demonstrate that the parishioners of Zácomil were storing weapons for the guerrillas.)

It was Epiphany, the Feast of the Three Kings, and the sanctuary was swarming with children. There were some wry comments as the three *gringos* ("wise men" from the *north?*) joined the congregation. I do not function easily under the guise of royalty, especially in another language, but between us we were able to communicate that if there is *any* place one might find the Christ-child on Epiphany in 1990, it would be in a place like Zácomil, where attention is focused on the teeming children and the need to create a safe future for them. "Let Christ's presence be found in the children" was the implicit message of the morning.

And then the mass ended. But it didn't really end. For

some of the women told us that if we wanted to understand the parish of Zácomil, it was not enough just to have gone to church. And so they took us to their cooperative, with the wonderful name of *El Paraíso* (which means just what it looks like it means). *El Paraíso* started out as a self-help program: families needed shelter, so they pooled their limited resources and acquired sufficient expertise to make concrete blocks for durable housing. After moving in, they knew a good thing when they saw it and started producing blocks for sale. "We may still be poor," one of the women said, "but we have our dignity, and we know we are all children of God." They are creating a tiny spot of "dignity" where they can live, and, even more importantly, where their children—those same children we saw at mass—can grow up with hope. So Epiphany ("manifestation") is not just one day a year in Zácomil, but a daily reality, a vote for a future that will have no room for another "slaughter of the innocents."

If you go far enough northwest from Managua, you will eventually come to the little Nicaraguan town of Ocotal, in the province of Nueva Segovia, just a few kilometers from the Honduran border. Being so close to the border made Ocotal a tempting target for the contras, since they could attack, flee into Honduras, and be immune from counterattack. Their strategy was to destroy places of storage for the harvested coffee crops, immobilize the radio station, destroy individual homes, and in the process kill male inhabitants, rape women inhabitants, and kidnap teenage male inhabitants to force them into military service against their own families. The younger children, not yet useful on the business end of a rifle, were still not immune from danger, as we found out

during a visit to the child-care center. We saw the usual
ditches and trenches around the school, but there was
another "defense" as well, and we saw it acted out.

Every now and then one of the teachers would come
into a room banging a pan loudly. This was a cue to the
children that it was time for the wonderful game of Fish.
Their part in the game was to lie down on the floor,
wherever they were, and, heads down and mouths open,
slither on their tummies into a central room described as
the "aquarium." Great fun.

What the children did not know, of course, was that
the game was deadly serious, and each posture had a
purpose. By lying down and keeping their heads low, the
children were less visible targets for sniper fire; by keeping their mouths open, they were protecting their ear-
drums from rupture by concussion, in case a bomb went
off close at hand; and by going to the central room, the
"aquarium," they were gathering in the one room that
had a reinforced roof, so that if the school sustained a
direct hit, the children might still survive.

When we got back to Managua after this sobering
experience we expressed our concern at the U.S. Embassy
that our tax dollars were being used to fund the contras in
ways that directly threatened the lives of innocent children. A member of the Embassy staff sought to put our
minds at rest. No problem, he said in effect. One of the
primary rules for winning in guerrilla warfare is to destroy
the "ideologues" of the next generation. He did not say,
but clearly implied, that the more the "ideologues" we
saw wiggling on the school floor were killed, the safer the
world would be for all of us. No problem.

Whenever I begin to feel complacent about the policies
of my government toward small countries, the children of

Ocotal come to view, wiggling along the floor, heads down, mouths open. I fear that a future generation of Americans will describe my generation of Americans as those who were willing to be the butchers of the children of the poor.

Only a shell is left of the cathedral in downtown Managua. The windows are gone, the roof is open to the sky, the pews, tables, and altar have long since disappeared. The cathedral was a victim not of the revolution of 1979 but of the earthquake of 1972.

The holiest place in a cathedral is supposed to be the altar, and upon the altar, the tabernacle housing the consecrated host that signals Christ's "real presence." In this ruined cathedral, however, there is no longer any vestige of holiness.

No, that is not quite true. For there is one place where holiness remains: part way up a pillar on the north side of the nave toward the back, someone has painted in red the subversive gospel slogan, *Paz y amor* (peace and love). Holiness indeed.

Chinks and cracks are multiplying in the cathedral walls. Someday the walls will come tumbling down like Jericho, either of their own accord or as the result of a demolition order trumpeted by church or government.

The collapse of the old cathedral will not signal the death of the church, however, nor will the building of a new cathedral necessarily signal its rebirth, for a new cathedral of garish design is already under construction in a more affluent part of town, far from the homes of the poor.

The message is clear: Do not look to the new building for the new life of the people of God. Look at the future through that old building, where tufts of grass are already growing up through the dirt in the chinks of the once-marble floor, a parable reminding us that the life of the church of the future will not be imposed from above. Rather it will arise out of the people—from below—as fresh and hopeful and tough as grass that has the power to crack marble.

1

A New Way of Understanding People

(the human side of God's story)

In the name of national security, individual insecurity is institutionalized.
—Archbishop Oscar Romero[1]

There is no neutral ground here. Either we serve the lives of Salvadorans, or we are accomplices in their death. And here we have the historical mediation of the very heart of our faith: either we believe in a God of life, or we serve the idols of death.
—Archbishop Romero, again

In beginning an exploration of liberation theology, it was important not to begin with concepts or principles or historical excursions, but to begin with *people*—people who live in very precarious circumstances, who put their lives on the line every day (and night) for their faith, and who live out the things about which I, for the most part, merely write. Some of the people whom the Introduction describes are friends; others I know about only at second hand; many are nameless, but no less dear to me.

When I hear the words "liberation theology," it is their faces that I see. When I hear, as I first heard many years ago, that my government has spent well over a decade either killing them or hiring others to kill them, I am sometimes sad and sometimes angry and usually both at the same time.

So it is not to score points in the theological world that

I write this book, but *to bear witness to my friends*, to let their story be told to people who might not otherwise hear it. I also write to keep reminding myself not only of their story but of their faith.

I want to know their secret.

My own faith, practiced in a situation of relative comfort, is challenged and threatened by what happens to them; their faith, on the contrary, seems to grow and deepen as they confront adversity. This is not a reason to leave them to confront adversity alone, but an invitation to join with them, in whatever ways are possible, to remove the sources of adversity, so that their lives can be fuller and—most important—so that the lives of their children can be free of starvation, terror, and premature death.

Making Connections

So if people are at the heart of it, how do we relate to Trinidad and Damos and Carmen and Medardo and Ignacio and Jon and Fernando and Ernesto and all the children of Zácomil and Ocotal? What points of connection are there, so that they can teach us?

For starters, here is another story. It does not take place thousands of miles away, but right here at home. It is located in Palo Alto, California, but it could just as well have happened—and probably has—in Duluth or Mobile or Bangor or Phoenix or Spokane.

Arlene has been a member of First Presbyterian Church for fifteen years. She has been active in lay leadership within the church. The particular vehicles of her service have been teaching Sunday school, working with youth with her husband, and facilitating a monthly Prayer

Group, open to all members, with a central core of people who have built up much trust in one another, and in the power of God in their lives.

Ten years ago another group in the church began meeting occasionally to think together about issues of social justice. The terrorism and exploitation in El Salvador at that time were prominent in their newspapers, and they kept returning to it again and again. As they became better informed, they realized that talk must move to action, and so they proposed that the church become a "sanctuary church," that is, willing to receive refugees from El Salvador or Guatemala who were fleeing out of fear that they would be killed for their political and religious opposition to a ruthless government. U.S. policy at the time was to round up all the "aliens" who had entered the United States illegally and ship them back to what often meant torture and death. It seemed inhuman. It *was* inhuman.

After much discussion, the session finally affirmed that First Presbyterian Church Palo Alto would become a "sanctuary church," even though it appeared to some members to be entering on a collision course with the law. For many members it was a scary undertaking, but the decision was widely supported.

Arlene was not particularly involved in public discussion of this issue, nor did she at the time have any real knowledge or special concern about it. The Prayer Group remained the center of her church life.

Within forty-eight hours of openly declaring "sanctuary," First Presbyterian Church suddenly had four young Salvadorans living in the church lounge. Dozens of members who had signed up ahead of time became involved in providing food, care, money, English lessons, and jobs

for Alvaro, José, Oscar, and Salvador, all the time won-
dering if the Immigration and Naturalization Service was
breathing down their necks and collecting data on them.

It was, to say the least, a consciousness-raising experience of a high order for middle-class church folk. Most
persevered, some burned out, and a few were transformed. None was more transformed than Arlene. Like
other members of the church, she had signed on earlier to
help out with the "refugees," and as she spent time with
them she began to get to know them. Salvador was a
student whose friends were being shot. Alvaro had been
photographed by the police putting up posters protesting
working conditions among the poor, so he was on a "list."
Oscar had joined the guerrilla forces and his wife and
baby had been killed by a land mine. José was at a labor
union demonstration when soldiers opened fire. He was
captured and tortured before being released.

The stories they told about themselves, and similar
ones they told about their friends and families still in El
Salvador, moved Arlene deeply, and with increasing clarity she realized that she was not dealing any more with a
concept, that is, "refugees," but with *persons*—Alvaro,
José, Oscar, and Salvador—persons who were hurting,
persons who needed support, persons who needed protection, persons who needed a place to take a shower,
persons who needed help, persons who needed hope,
simply because they were persons, on whose behalf
Christ had delivered a heavy mandate for his followers:
"Inasmuch as you do it to one of the least of these my
brothers and sisters, you do it unto me" (Matt. 25:40,
author's translation).

I do not hesitate to call Arlene's shift of perspective a
"conversion experience." It turned around the direction of

her life (which is what "con-version" means), and it turned around the priorities that were guiding it. She did not forsake the monthly Prayer Group, which now had a whole new agenda of concerns, but she found herself doing many other things as well: finding clothing and housing and shoes and jobs and English teachers for Alvaro, José, Oscar, and Salvador. As the initial zeal of other church members tapered off, Arlene's zeal increased. She took a crash course in Spanish in Guatemala and then visited El Salvador herself, returning with new commitment. She organized letter-writing campaigns and telephone trees to Washington, protesting our support of the Salvadoran army and our denial of legal status to those who were trying to flee from the army and the "death squads."

At the end of each Sunday morning's worship, the congregation of First Presbyterian Church Palo Alto gathers around the communion table for prayers and "calls to action." And the best symbol for me of what happened to Arlene is that instead of calling attention only to the monthly Prayer Group, she began to say things like: "There's going to be a rally on the steps of the City Hall in San Jose at noon on Thursday to protest the returning of Salvadoran refugees—and we all have to be there." This can also be called praying with one's feet.

The story goes on. Arlene recently made arrangements for a husband and wife, victims of torture, to come from El Salvador to the church, and they lived in her home for several months while making the initial adjustment to a new culture. But the continually important thing about her "conversion" is the deeply rooted commitment to *persons*, who, after all, are far more important than concepts. So if we are going to find a "point of connection" between Latin Americans and ourselves, this is where it will be found: in a new recognition that what goes on far away (or near at hand) is important to us because *persons are being violated and destroyed*.

Not everyone has the privilege I have had of knowing some of these persons in their own situations. Not everybody has had the privilege Arlene has had in knowing them in her own situation. But this does not deprive any of us of the obligation to attempt to create such contacts, and to engage in acts of consecrated imagination by which we, too, wherever we are, can at least begin to understand what their experiences have been, and what an obligation those experiences place on us, who have so often been complacent spectators of our own government's support of evil and our own inaction in the face of it.

The Human Story and God's Story

The subtitle of this chapter is "the human side of God's story." So far, the name of God has appeared infrequently in these pages. It will appear more frequently in the pages to come, as we begin to realize that a God so often "hidden" from us is manifestly present in the lives and situations of the poor in many ways, if only we have the imagination and the courage to look there. When a death squad kills, God is being mocked. When an inhabitant of Paiwas takes risks for others, God is at work. When a child is starving, those who permit it to starve are self-defined as nonbelievers. When a mother gives food to her children even when there is none left for her, God is present in that kitchen, or the outdoor shed that passes for a kitchen. When Ita Ford, Maura Clarke, Dorothy Kazel, and Jean Donovan work with "the poorest of the poor" in El Salvador, and are raped and shot as a result, the crucifixion of Jesus Christ is being reenacted in our own time. God is present in the anguish as well as in the hope.

We do not have the power single-handedly to turn anguish into hope. But together, in community, we can make a difference.

Whenever we deny that, we should be shamed by the fact that those whom Jesus identified as "the very least of these my brothers [and sisters]," refuse to succumb to such a sense of powerlessness. They keep hope alive in refugee camps like Colomoncagua, in small villages like Ocotal and Paiwas, in the barrios of Managua and San Salvador, in the "base communities" all over the place, where (as we will see) hope is anchored in the ongoing power of the biblical story of a God who dwells not somewhere else, but in the very midst of where God's people are. And when there is no hope, they invent hope.

Such change is not the product of idle dreaming. It comes out of their earthy contact with "good news to the poor"—the center of Jesus' agenda—which assures them that God does not want poverty to remain their lot, and that once they realize that and begin working together to do battle against poverty, all sorts of divine resources will be unleashed. They are becoming, in a favorite phrase, "subjects of their own history," rather than mere objects that can be manipulated and destroyed by anyone who cares to do so, and has a few guns at his disposal.

Let us make no mistake. They are "the human side of God's story," and their liberation has already begun.

Four Recurring Themes

That is a quick overview of some of the themes in the following pages. For the rest of this chapter, we will highlight four of the ways in which God's people are understood in those parts of the Latin American church that have been impacted by liberation theology.

Compromiso

The key word is *compromiso*. This is a much misunderstood word in North America because it looks so much like our word *compromise*, suggesting adjustments and "deals" to avoid confrontation. But its meaning in Spanish is just the opposite. *Compromiso* means "commitment," taking a stand, being so clear about what is really important that thought and action cannot be separated. Many times, indeed, the actions are the real content of the *compromiso*, and intellectualizing about them comes much later, if at all. In a phrase out of our own culture, *compromiso* means something like "putting your body where your words are."

We saw a good example of *compromiso* in responses to the story of the killing of the Jesuits, their housekeeper, and her daughter. Ordinary logic, we recall, goes: Ignacio was killed for speaking out; therefore we had better not speak out or we will be killed too. But a response based on *compromiso* would go: Ignacio was killed for speaking out; therefore we must take his place and speak out too.

Our choices in North America are likely to be less stark and dramatic, but they can similarly challenge us: Arthur has risked getting fired for challenging the racial policies of his corporation: therefore (a) we had better not be seen associating with him, or (b) we must stand with him and support him.

A good test of *compromiso* is the degree of concern it engenders for children. One of the underground groups in Chile had, as its vision of the future, the slogan, *Y los únicos privilegiados seran los niños,* "and the only privileged ones will be the children." It is amazing and heartening to see how central children are to life in Latin America, and it is amazing and disheartening to see how desperate is the plight of so many of those children—born into a world in which they are more than likely to be victims of malnutrition, ongoing hunger, lack of education, fear, and a dozen other perils. The content of *compromiso* almost always has concern for children at its center: "It will take time to produce change. If we do not enjoy its results in our lifetime, let them at least be available for our children."

So in the future, the "privileged" will not be the rich, nor even those who have made it above the poverty line and cling there precariously. No one will be "privileged" . . . except the children. A useful yardstick for measuring social advance can always be, "What does it do for the lives of children?"

We have it on high authority that the kingdom of God is like a little child. Any human approximation of it had better reflect that.

Hope

The driving force behind *compromiso*—the commitment of the whole person to a better future—is surely *hope*. This must be emphasized because, while hope can come easily to us in our relatively comfortable situations, it is one of the last things in the world we would expect to find in most parts of Latin America, where poverty, oppression, disease, and premature death are the order of the day. What sustains hope?

Gustavo Gutiérrez, a parish priest in a poor area of Lima, Peru, puts it this way: People come down to Latin America and they see all the poverty, all the suffering, all the oppression, and they think, "How sad! how terrible!" And they are right; it *is* sad and terrible. But they are failing to see one thing. For the first time in their history, poor people can begin to have hope, for they are discovering that things do not have to remain the way they are. *Change is possible.* That has never been part of the life of the poor until recently. They thought that they were fated to remain just as they were. Indeed, it was the message of the church for hundreds of years that things would *not* _hange, and that one's task on earth was simply to accept wherever one was on the social-economic scale as God's will. But now the poor are discovering that it cannot truly be God's will for most of God's children to suffer. God wills life and love and fullness for all and not just a few. And God wants our help to bring that about.[2]

An important and unexpected result of this has been the emergence of what can be called "the joy of the poor." Comfortable North Americans had better be chary about using the phrase, for it can easily lead to an attitude that goes, "If the poor are really joyful, let them remain that way." But Latin Americans themselves point out that even in the midst of poverty (not because of it) there can be joy. There are fiestas, celebrations, songs, religious ceremonies, that, while not ignoring past indignities, celebrate future possibilities, and thus transform the present into a time of joyful anticipation of what is to come. The Gospel of Luke reports that "those who suffer today shall laugh tomorrow," and the transforming dynamic behind this claim is that, when it is grasped, *tomorrow has begun today.*

There have been many martyrs and there will surely be many more—people who die for their faith. But even the martyrs instill hope, for their causes do not languish but are carried on by others. And, as Gutiérrez points out further, there is probably nothing that more deeply worries those with power than the fact that the poor can laugh. That the poor can weep is what the powerful expect, and they can cope with that. But the *laughter* of the poor? How does one account for that? What dreadful secret, what power for change, does it portend?

God's presence

Is there any grounding for this commitment and this hope? Are they anything but wishful thinking, making the best of a bad situation?

The answer is not hard to find. The reason for strong *compromiso* and deeply grounded hope is that the people recognize that they are not alone, that *God is in their midst*—God working with them, and calling on them to work with God. "The human side of God's story" has two meanings here: (1) God's presence manifested in many other persons, and (2) God's presence manifested in a particular person, Jesús de Nazarét.

As we have already seen, signs of God are visible whenever one person puts his or her life on the line for a friend; whenever people put concerns for others' safety above concern for their own safety; whenever those who have little enough for themselves share with those who have even less. In such events we can see revealed the kind of love that is grounded in the very nature of the universe.

But in addition, there is a special human life in which the immediate presence of God is experienced. For the center of liberation faith—and all Christian faith—is that God was present in a unique way in the life of this Jesús de Nazarét, one who was fully human like the rest of us (whatever more we may later affirm about him). Faith has often blunted this fact of Jesus' full humanity, and depicted him exclusively as sitting on a throne in heaven, or otherwise being exempted from the frustrations of the daily grind. But for those who have seen Jesus through the new lens provided by liberation theology, a different picture begins to emerge. Jesus, in sharing our humanity, did not do so as a king or a royal potentate or as part of the ruling class of society; he did so as one who was born into, and lived among, the poor himself. He identified with the outcast because he was one of them. His habitation was among those who were called the *am-ha'aretz*, the poor of the land, those who had no privileges or rights. He had no formal education beyond what anyone else in that time would have had. Furthermore, he was a Jew, a practicing member of a community of people who were virtually religious outcasts. The stories reported about his birth indicate that he would have been considered illegitimate, a terrible stigma in the culture of the time, and most other cultures since then.

But even with such unprepossessing credentials, he made a mighty impact. He spoke of bringing "good news to the poor," and his agenda included concern for those in prison, those who were slaves, those who were victimized by life around them. So radical and unsettling was his message that he lasted no more than three years on the public scene and probably less, by which time those with power perceived him as such a threat that they did away with him through a phony trial and a judicial murder.

The claim is that in *that* life, God was present in our midst. That is not the kind of God to whom North Americans instinctively turn. But if God *is* such a God, it is clear that such a God would embody very good news to the poor and oppressed—a God who takes sides with them, who identifies with them in the midst of their poverty and oppression. If they feel "despised and rejected," so did he. If they get hungry and discouraged, so did he. If they feel betrayed by their friends, so was he. If they would like a sense that better things are in store, he fortifies that hope. If they need an assurance that violent death is not the end of their friends and loved ones, the story of his resurrection is a story that transforms their own stories from despair to hope.

That there should have been such a human life is itself good news. That in such a human life God was uniquely present is the best news of all, and in response to it a new level of *compromiso* and hope are possible. Here is one who is indeed, "the God of the poor."

Preferential option for the poor

Compromiso, hope, God "in the midst"—these themes converge on one more, with which we can draw it all together. Again and again in the lives of Latin Americans we hear references to *a preferential option for the poor*. We are told that the *Bible* indicates God making a preferential option for the poor. Religious leaders proclaim that the *church* must make a preferential option for the poor. The phrase has its critics (who usually misunderstand its true meaning), but it has persistently made its way into the literature and, much more important, the lives of those who try to embody a theology of liberation.

A clarification: many people assume that the phrase is the equivalent of making "an *exclusive* option for the poor"—as though God loved only the poor and hated the rich. (This is one reason well-off folks tend to look askance at the phrase. Too threatening.) The gospel, of course, proclaims that God loves *all* people, not just some. But when we observe that in God's world the poor get a decidedly unfair share of the world's goods (due chiefly to human greed), the fact that God does love *all* means that there must be food, shelter, jobs, and humane living conditions for all and not just for some. To create a situation of "liberty and justice for all," then, it is necessary to start to make some changes, and the phrase we are examining asserts that we must start with the poor—that is, make an "option" on their behalf. This means that when a legislative proposal is under discussion, or a plan for a social program is being floated, the question to ask is, "Will this, or will this not, improve the situation of the poor?" If it will, it should be supported, since it will bring about a consequent broadening of the degree of social justice in society. If it will not, it should be opposed, since it will simply entrench the nonpoor with greater power than ever.

The opposite of a preferential option for the *poor* would be a preferential option for the *rich,* assuming that if the rich get more and more money and goods, some of the gains will "trickle down" to the poor. This is a convenient theory for the well-to-do, but it is a dubious bit of psychology and economics, since those with wealth are exceedingly loath to share it with others, and the result of a preferential option for the rich is almost always that the rich get richer while the poor get poorer.

So for the sake of *all,* and not just for the sake of some, "a preferential option for the poor" provides a guideline for the kinds of change that are necessary to bring greater justice into an unjust world. Clearly, attempts to close the gap between rich and poor are part of the mandate of the gospel, and those who find such proposals threatening need to reflect on the fact that the notion of a preferential option for the poor is not just the newest theory to come from radical economists, but is the clear thrust of the biblical message. Literally hundreds of verses in the scriptures talk about God as "the God of the poor"; about the duty of all people to have a special concern for "widows and orphans," since they are the most disadvantaged and powerless people in the ancient world; about the warnings of the prophets to the rich who misuse their wealth; and about the duty of all people toward the economically deprived. These are not just "social" or "economic" concerns. They are biblical, Christian, and "religious" concerns.

It is not hard to see how such a message rings a responsive cord in the lives and hearts of the two thirds of the human family who go to bed hungry every night, or the parents who fear that their child will be one of the fifteen thousand children who die every day from starvation or malnutrition. If we were truly hungry, we would have greater sympathy for those who are, and realize that any God of love worthy of the name is as concerned about the state of their stomachs as about the state of their souls.

Not a bad starting point for us.

2

A New Way of Seeing the World

(1492 and all that)

A sacrifice from ill-gotten gains is tainted,
and the gifts of the wicked win no approval.
The Most High has no pleasure in the offerings of the
    godless,
nor do countless sacrifices win his forgiveness.
To offer a sacrifice from the possessions of the poor
is like killing a son before his father's eyes.
Bread is life to the destitute,
and to deprive them of it is murder.
To rob your neighbour of his livelihood is to kill him,
and he who defrauds a worker of his wages sheds
    blood.

> Ecclesiasticus 34:18–22, the passage that
> "converted" Bartolomé de las Casas

What good are beautiful highways and airports, all
these beautiful skyscrapers, if they are fashioned out of
the clotted blood of the poor who will never enjoy
them?

> —Archbishop Romero

If you are standing at the top of a high sand dune on the
ocean shore, you may see a ship on the horizon. If, at the
same moment, someone is standing at the bottom of
the dune, right on the shore line, that person will not see
the ship at all; it will be "over the horizon" and therefore
out of sight.

This truth is obvious when we are dealing with consequences of the curvature of the earth's surface: *where we*

stand determines what we see. It is less obvious, but equally true, when we are dealing with ideology rather than geography, with the convictions people hold about the world and themselves: *where we stand determines not only what we see but, even more importantly, what we want.*

If you "stand" in a situation of affluence, you want the legislature to lower the income tax rate for the rich, and cut out the capital gains tax altogether. If you "stand" in a situation of poverty, you want some of the goods of this world made available to you. You think a graduated income tax is a dandy idea, and you are unpersuaded by a logic asserting that if the rich are allowed to keep more of their money, more will trickle down to the poor.

A British writer in London saw two women in fourth-floor flats on opposite sides of a narrow street arguing violently with each other. He commented, in a display of subtle British humor, "They will never agree. They are arguing from different premises." This is true of many of our verbal tiffs: We are arguing from different premises or presuppositions, and since the premises differ drastically, agreement is always hard to reach.

Different Ways of Using the Past

In no area of life, perhaps, is this more apparent than in what we do with history. Calvinists and Catholics have different appraisals of the Protestant Reformation, since they approach it with different presuppositions. British and American historians have different interpretations of the American Revolution, for the same reason. We have only recently emerged from a yearlong national "celebration" of the five hundredth anniversary of the "discovery" of America by Christopher Columbus. And before we put away the banners and slogans for another five hundred years, it will be worthwhile to reflect on the arguments, from different "premises," that were offered to explain the importance of Columbus's voyage, since they have a direct bearing on how we understand liberation theology today, and the degree to which we are open to it. Two very conflicting interpretations emerged during the year of "celebration."

The first can be called *the cheerleading version*, and it offered a very attractive scenario. The fact that "In fourteen hundred and ninety-two, Columbus sailed the ocean blue" illustrated that he was a bold adventurer engaging in a very brave act by sailing into unchartered waters, testing a radical theory that by sailing west one could go east, and taking the not inconsiderable risk that he and his whole company might simply fall off the edge of the earth. But he survived all those hazards, found a "New World" inhabited by Indians with whom he generously shared the great benefits of Western Civilization, including (as recorded in the Sunday school version of the tale) the Christian religion, so that the salvation of the immortal souls of the Indians could be guaranteed. Not to be sneezed at was a further happy by-product: he found gold and brought large amounts of it back to Europe so that his investors and their friends could reap handsome profits.

But there is a second version of the Columbus story that can be called *the debunking version*. It is the product of Native Americans, African Americans, Latin American Indians, and other groups who have their own reasons for seeing Columbus's arrival in the West Indies as a disaster rather than a triumph. Since it is a less familiar version, we must explore it more fully. It goes something like this:

To begin with, the cheerleaders' starting point is

flawed. The real "discovery" of America took place about twenty thousand years earlier than Columbus, when itinerant Asian tribes crossed the Bering Strait and traveled down the land mass we now know as North, Central, and South America, establishing indigenous cultures with a high degree of civilization, still visible in Mayan ruins, Aztec art, Native American tribal life, and so on. About nineteen thousand years later, beginning in 1492, the land of these indigenous peoples was invaded and the inhabitants decimated. The arrival of Columbus started a wholesale massacre that went on for centuries.

The individual who initiated these baleful events, Christopher Columbus, is far from the exemplary character most white historians have described. He was destructive and greedy. Having gotten to the "Indies," he went from island to island demanding gold from the inhabitants on pain of death (frequently killing them in groups of thirteen—twelve for the Apostles and one more for the Redeemer), and he took many Indians back to Spain as slaves for the wealthy. Rape of Indian women by members of his company was routine. When he was made Colonial Administrator of the Indies he botched the job badly, even in the eyes of the Spaniards who appointed him.

More destructive than the impact of Columbus himself, however, was the legacy of conquest he bequeathed to his followers. He set up patterns of exploitation in the "new world" that enabled the Spanish conquistadors, armed military "conquerors," to spread throughout the Caribbean, Central America, and the west coast of South America, claiming as their own whatever they fancied—women, gold, artifacts, mines, forests—and routinely killing or torturing any Indians foolhardy enough to stand in their way.

This laid the groundwork for policies followed through half a millennium that can only be described as *genocide*— the slaughter of entire races and tribes of people. When the Indian population as a consequence dipped to a fragment of what it had been, the conquistadors started bringing shipload after shipload of blacks from Africa to be slaves, under terrible conditions that not even the most sanitized versions of the story can hide. The overwhelming aim of the conquistadors was to get gold, gold, gold, and in the name of that god they found ways to justify whatever they wanted to do.

On the basis of these realities, the debunkers have asserted (I believe rightly) that the five hundredth anniversary of the first of Columbus's voyages should have been an occasion for penitence rather than celebration, and for a decision to try to right some of the wrongs the "invasion" produced.

So we have two very different interpretations of the same event, one highly supportive, the other deeply challenging. These two interpretations, however, do not exhaust our ways of looking at the world today in the light of 1492. There is a contemporary of Columbus who provides an almost perfect foil for him and furnishes a creative alternative for us in further reflection on the issues we have been examining. His name, Bartolomé de las Casas, is hardly a household word, but for reasons that will become apparent, he deserves to become one.[1]

Learning from Las Casas

Bartolomé de las Casas was nine years old when Columbus made his historic voyage. His father went on Columbus's second trip and came back with a souvenir for his son—an Indian to be his very own slave. As he grew up, Las Casas himself felt the lure of the "Indies" and after some education went himself to teach Christian doctrine to the natives. After a trip back to Europe to prepare for the priesthood, he returned to the New World. He worked closely enough with the authorities (helping, for example, to put down native rebellions) so that he was twice given an *encomienda*. The *encomienda* was a clever device designed to help the conquistadors simultaneously achieve affluence and accrue credit in heaven. Large tracts of land (along with whatever Indians were living on them) were given to Spaniards in gratitude for services rendered. The owners could extract forced labor from the indigenous squatters, especially to dig for gold—hence the affluence. In return, the owners of the *encomiendas* promised to teach the gospel to the heathen Indians so that they could die in a state of grace and thus escape damnation—hence the accrued credit in heaven for those who made this possible. It was a splendid arrangement for people like Las Casas, although its merits were less apparent to the Indians.

Priest and landowner rolled in one, Las Casas lived as an affluent *encomendero* for about twelve years. He apparently felt no personal pangs of conscience, though he was increasingly uneasy as he saw fellow landowners ruthlessly exploiting their workers and torturing and killing those who consistently made trouble. The matter came to a head for Las Casas in 1514. As he was preparing to preach on Pentecost, he was bowled over by a passage in Ecclesiasticus—the passage reproduced at the beginning of this chapter. A genuine "conversion experience" followed. Each phrase of the passage became a lance, sharp-pointed and devastating: the sins the author was describing were the sins of Las Casas. He had "ill-gotten gains" accumulated by the slave-labor practices on the *encomiendas* (v. 18); when he "offered a sacrifice" it was indeed "from the possessions of the poor" that he had unjustly appropriated (vs. 19–20); by depriving his workers of sufficient food he had to confront the claim that such deprivation was "murder" (v. 21); the whole *encomienda* system was designed "to rob your neighbor of his livelihood," which meant, very simply, "to kill him" (v. 22); and, most searing of all, the conclusion that "he who defrauds a worker of his wages sheds blood" (v. 22).

Las Casas felt the sting of indictment on every score and also realized that if he was indicted, so was every *encomendero* in the new world. He preached his new conviction to fellow owners who were very surprised and not the least pleased; no one followed his example of giving up his *encomienda*. So Las Casas went back to Spain to seek help from the king and get some rules and regulations that would root out brutality against the Indians. Some alternative schemes were devised with royal approval but were unsuccessful when moved from the realm of theory propounded in Spain to the realm of practice worked out in the Indies.

For a number of years Las Casas went into a kind of retirement, becoming a novice in the Dominican order. But he was not temperamentally attuned to disengagement. His ideas began to attract public attention and some of them even made their way into a papal bull, emphasizing the Las Casas contention that Indians were fully human, not subhuman or "talking animals," and that they deserved the same treatment as that accorded everyone else. In a book written for King Charles V, called *The Devastation of the Indies,* Las Casas documented what was going on. He did not mince words:

> [The conquistadors] are still acting like ravening beasts,
> killing, terrorizing, afflicting, torturing, and destroying
> the native peoples. . . . [T]he Christians have an ulti-
> mate aim, which is to acquire gold. . . .[T]heir insatia-
> ble greed and ambition, the greatest ever seen in the
> world, is the cause of their villainies.[2]

The king was impressed by the evidence, and sweeping
reforms were passed. Las Casas went back to implement
them as bishop of Chiapas, Mexico. He not only attacked
the *encomienda* system but the owners as well. He asserted
that they were living in mortal sin, and that they would
remain in that state until they got rid of their holdings and
paid adequate reparations to the Indians they had exploited. Only after that could they expect to be absolved
and go to mass again.

Such a hard line was not calculated to win friends and
influence people, and after being ridiculed, disobeyed,
called a traitor, and even a "Lutheran," Las Casas went
back to Spain and spent the rest of his life in court working
for the rights of Indians. "His is a candle," one opponent
wrote in warning, "that will set everything on fire." Another, paying him tribute, described him as "an Old Testament prophet and canon lawyer combined"—a formidable
combination, as anyone who has ever known either a
prophet or a canon lawyer will readily understand.

The story of Las Casas furnishes us with tools that will
be useful during the rest of this study. First, Las Casas
made clear that the central motivation of the conquistadors was greed—greed for gold, a greed so great that gold
became their god. The new god of our own day may be
spelled o-i-l, but the dynamics are the same.

Second, the Las Casas way of thinking theologically
presages what we find in liberation theology today. In a

famous debate with another theologian, Juan Ginés Sepúlveda, he did not start with abstract principles (such as that Indians are "inferior" creatures because Aristotle said so) but with the immediate human situation of living and dying Indians, possessing the full rational capacity of human beings, who could therefore not be treated as subhuman (as Sepúlveda argued), but were entitled to the same respect accorded all others.

Third, where others categorized the Indians as "heathen" and "infidels," Las Casas viewed them in gospel terms as "the poor" for whom God has a special concern, and to whom, therefore, a ministry of love must be extended. "Better a live Indian even though an infidel," he reasoned, "than a dead Indian even though a Christian."

Fourth, Las Casas's view of Christ was formed out of such a starting point and engagement. "In the Indies," he wrote upon returning to Spain, "I left behind Jesus Christ, our God, suffering affliction, scourging and crucifixion, not once but thousands of times." He spoke more frequently of "the scourged Christ of the Indies" than of the triumphant Christ ruling on a heavenly throne.

Fifth, Las Casas insisted, particularly to the owners of the *encomiendas*, that they were jeopardizing their salvation by their treatment of the Indians: "It is impossible for someone to be saved if he does not observe justice."

Sixth, for Las Casas faith grew out of being a *participant* with oppressed people in their struggle, rather than a detached *observer* located somewhere else.

A New Starting Point—And Three Follow-ups

In one way, the earlier analogy of the sand dune and the horizon fails us. It assumes that the view from the top is *better* than the view from the bottom—more inclusive, more accurate. But what the liberation theologians are telling us is that the *true* view is "the view from below," from what they call "the underside of history." People who read a book like this one see the world, for the most part, from above, from a privileged position, available only to a few, and therefore with an elitist perspective, whereas what is truly going on for the great majority of the human family can be seen only from below, at ground level, from within the crushing weight of poverty, malnutrition, oppression, sickness, and death.

If where we stand does determine what we see, we must make an effort, however doomed to ultimate failure, to stand where we can see what others see. What does the world look like to them?

With whatever differences, they all share at least one overriding conviction: *the world they see should not be the way it is*. It does not take a theological degree or a lot of sophistication or years of graduate study to learn that. It takes only some years of living. If it is not self-evident, it can never be demonstrated. Juan Luis Segundo, a Jesuit from Uruguay, warns us that unless we agree that the world should not be the way it is, we can never understand what liberation theology is all about. If we are satisfied with the world as it is, there is no point of contact, because the world that is satisfying to us is the same world that is utterly devastating to them.

It is hard to accept such an analysis if the world *has* been kind to us, and we have never experienced hunger or torture or even insolvency. But we must accept Segundo's challenge. What else *must* we see?

At least three things are involved for us in a new way of

seeing the world, if we try to take "the view from below" seriously.

Social analysis

The first of these is to use the tools of social analysis in order to understand the world better than we have in the past. Instead of reading only philosophers (a favorite indoor sport of theologians) in order to *understand* the world, Latin American Christians are taking seriously the insights of social scientists, sociologists, and economists, in order to learn how to *change* the world. That in itself is an insight from a controversial "social scientist," Karl Marx, who wrote, "The philosophers have only interpreted the world in different ways; the point is to change it." One need not be a Marxist to resonate to such a statement. Clearly, if one wants to change the world, one should know as much as possible about how it works, how power is accumulated and challenged, and how social structures can be realigned to serve the cause of justice rather than injustice.

The word that Paulo Freire, a Brazilian sociologist, has coined to describe this process is *conscientization*, or, as we might more easily say, "consciousness raising," becoming aware of things we hadn't noticed before.[3] To take but one example, consciousness raising involves discovering that evil not only is present in the hearts of powerful individuals who muck things up for the rest of us but is embedded in the very structures of society, so that those structures, and not just individuals who work within them, must be changed if the world is to change.

Gustavo Gutiérrez, who is perhaps the foremost liberation theologian, and to whom we have already referred, has analyzed this in relation to poverty.[4] He has discovered three things:

(a) Poverty is *destructive*. One can never be romantic about it, as Christians sometimes are. It must be fought against and destroyed. It cannot be eliminated simply by occasional acts of charity, which assuage the consciences of the rich and provide temporary relief for the poor but do nothing to transform the basic situation of the poor.

(b) Poverty is not accidental but *structural*. It is built into the way society is organized. It is advantageous, for example, for industry to have a large and permanent pool of unemployed workers, who, in their immediate needs for self and family, will bid against each other to work for exceedingly low wages, thereby increasing the margin of profit of the owners. Full employment would actually be disadvantageous in such a society.

(c) The victims of poverty are a *social class*. They tend to be discriminated against and manipulated so that they become little more than objects, expendable at the workplace when they get tired or sick. The other side of this insight, however, is that when a social class becomes self-conscious about its needs, its members can band together, organize, and begin to demand greater justice in society as a whole.[5]

Seeking change

If such analysis is taken seriously, and enough people reflect upon it, the possibility of change will begin to be taken seriously, with the resultant question: *How is change to be brought about?* There are two basic answers.

The first is to seek *change from above*, which is what a word like "super-version" would literally mean. Those in charge, on top, propose changes so that the present benefits to themselves will remain, with perhaps a little less injustice overall; or, more likely, those not on top put pressure on those who *are* on top to make certain changes—pay better wages, perhaps, or provide better health conditions in the factory. This may work to a degree, but the built-in reality is that pressures from below will be resisted if they threaten the survival of social structures that bring substantial benefits to those on top. Such changes as are achieved are likely to be little more than cosmetic and token.

Such frustrations are likely to lead to a second approach, *change from below,* which is what the word "subversion" literally means. Let us acknowledge that the word "subversion" immediately raises scary images. We have been conditioned to react strongly against anyone who is labeled "subversive" and to be fearful of anything labeled a "subversive organization." Such things are "anti-American" if not "terrorist."

Let us try to put such pictures aside for the moment, and consider the word "subversion" simply as a description of poor people working at the grass roots, who discover that they are being exploited and are entitled to more than an unjust society is offering them. The strategy is, in effect, "Don't agonize, organize." Such people do not want to rule the world or liquidate the upper middle class. They *do* want sufficient food for their children, adequate housing for their families, a chance for further education themselves, and appropriate clothing to protect them in inclement weather.

These are not exorbitant demands. They are things to which every human being has a *right,* and if large num-

bers of people are denied such rights, it makes moral
sense for them to organize and exert pressure on those
who have the resources to make life more equitable for all.
This may mean holding public hearings, attending
marches and rallies to call attention to their concerns,
organizing labor unions where there have been none,
voting defenders of the status quo out of office, and (if
none of those things work) moving on to strikes, sit-ins,
work stoppages, and so forth. (Only at the far end of such
a continuum, "when all else fails," is the option of violence really relevant, and in the kinds of situations being
discussed, the option of violence is almost always initiated by those who already *have* the power, rather than by
those who do not.)

Belief in the kingdom of God

All kinds of people, whether Christian or not, can
participate in the kind of social analysis undertaken
above. But Christians bring a further resource, important
to them not only in clarifying their goals but in suggesting
means of attaining them. This is their belief in the biblical
notion of *the kingdom of God*. The discovery of the Bible has
been a tremendous catalyst for change in Latin America.
As a persistent theme in the Hebrew scriptures, and a
central concern in Jesus' parables, the kingdom of God
presents an alternative picture—God's vision of what the
world could be—a world in which justice flourishes, compassion abounds, and concern for the poor is paramount.

But we need to be very clear: in the Bible, the kingdom
of God is always pictured as a *gift*—God's gift—rather
than a human attainment. On human beings, however, is
placed the task of "preparing the way" for the coming of

the kingdom, seeking to destroy barriers to its coming, and initiating activities and attitudes that will help people to be citizens of the kingdom when God does initiate it.

Jesus' sermon in Nazareth, built on a passage from the prophet Isaiah, sets out some of the characteristics of the kingdom: there will be "good news to the poor," freedom to the captives, recovery of sight to the blind, liberation to the oppressed, and the inauguration of the "jubilee year," a concept present in the Hebrew scriptures, in which present injustice and indignities will be overcome and a new start made possible. Jesus declares not only that this is his own agenda, but even announces that it is *already* in process of being realized (see Luke 4:16–21).

Alongside the imagery of the kingdom, but distinct from it, is the dream of a *utopia*, a humanly constructed better world. So, while very different from the notion of the kingdom of God, the notion of utopia sometimes operates in tandem with it as part of the dream of oppressed persons—human proposals for a new society that include fairness for all and exclude special privileges for the few. Francis Bacon and Thomas More made such proposals. Some thinkers create dystopias, or negative visions, that model societies of the future to be avoided, such as Aldous Huxley's *Brave New World* or George Orwell's *1984*.

It is clear that total commitment to the kingdom of God, and provisional commitment to utopian models, can inspire people to challenge the way things are. As long as they are not confused with one another, they can provide a "vision" for the future—a theme often derided by our national political leaders, but essential for oppressed peoples. It is simply a descriptive reality that "where there is no vision, the people perish" (Prov. 29:18, KJV).

Today, to a degree unparalleled in their history, oppressed peoples are realizing not only that "the world should not be the way it is" but that *the world need not remain the way it is*. It could be different. It could be better. And if people work together on utopian possibilities, reinforced by their recognition that God also wills a better future for them and that they can "prepare the way" for the gift of God's kingdom—then new things can happen.

3

A New Way of Encountering God

("to know God is to do justice")

> In the name of God, then, in the name of this suffering
> people, whose screams and cries mount to heaven, and
> daily grow louder, I beg you, I entreat you, I order you
> in the name of God: stop the repression!
> —Archbishop Romero's last public words, addressed
>   to the Salvadoran army and the "death squads"

Start with an image provided by Henri Nouwen, a Dutch priest who spent a year in Latin America determining whether he had a "call" to stay there and work with the poor. He is writing in the middle of Ronald Reagan's first term as president of the United States.

> There is a little man in Peru, a man without any power,
> who lives in a *barrio* with poor people and who wrote a
> book. In this book he simply reclaimed the basic Chris-
> tian truth that God became human to bring good news
> to the poor, new light to the blind, and liberty to the
> captives. Ten years later this book and the movement it
> started are considered dangerous by [the United States
> of America] the greatest power on earth. When I look at
> this little man, Gustavo [Gutiérrez], and think about the
> tall Ronald Reagan, I see David standing before Goli-
> ath, again with no more weapon than a little stone, a
> stone called *A Theology of Liberation*.[1]

How strange that the leader of "the greatest power on earth" should be frightened by a book. And yet it is true that Mr. Reagan, and the U.S. Department of State, and leaders of the armed forces of "the greatest power on earth" met several times and wrote secret documents to one another about how best to neutralize the influence not only of a book on liberation theology, but even more "the movement it started."

And how strange that Henri Nouwen should believe that the power of "the movement it started" might be stronger than the power of the United States—which is the only conclusion that his cast of characters (David and Goliath) will allow us to draw.

We can be sure that if Gustavo Gutiérrez and liberation theology had been concerned only about heaven, there would have been no scurryings of perturbation on the part of those who worked in the White House or Foggy Bottom or the Pentagon. A theology that was no more than a soothing otherworldly tranquilizer would have suited them splendidly, for then they could have gone about their business sure that no challenges to their use (or abuse) of earthly power would be forthcoming.

But liberation theology doesn't fit the mold. It is assuredly about God and the church and Jesus Christ and salvation and the sacraments and all the other things theologians write about. But it insists that all those topics must be planted in the firm soil of the earth (which God happens to have created), and that therefore many things that are happening on that same earth have to be challenged, judged, overthrown . . . and replaced. Indeed (as we shall see), the starting point for liberation theology is not all the topics theologians write about, but the here-and-nowness of what is happening on street corners or at soup kitchens or in the far-reaching decisions made by politicians and generals, such as "Shall we go to war or not?" and "How do we remain Number One in relation to Germany and Japan?"

The fact that so far in this book, which is presumably about God, we have said little *directly* about God (save for a couple of pages toward the end of the previous chapter), is something that has been done deliberately in order to be faithful to the basic approach of liberation theology. And the fact that from here on we shall think more directly about God is a similar attempt to be faithful to our subject matter.

Whenever we speak about God we are "doing theology"—a phrase that frightens many people since it sounds so esoteric. The simplest translation of the Greek word *theo-logia* is "God-talk," or, a little more elegantly, "discourse about God." And since we all talk about God in one way or another, we are all theologians. We may be good theologians or bad theologians, but theologians we are, whatever adjective we put before the word.

What kind of theologians, then, are liberation theologians? How do they "encounter" God? What distinguishes them from other theologians so that they bring hope to the poor and fear to the mighty? We will be as tidy as the unkempt discipline of theology allows, and examine six characteristics of liberation theology, making lavish use of the insights of the foremost liberation theologian, Gustavo Gutiérrez.

Theology as a Love Letter

So that we do not start too pompously, let us begin with an image from Gutiérrez: theology is a love letter to God, to the church, and to the people.[2] It is not so much a formally manageable series of propositions ("There are four attributes of God"; "There are five theories of the atonement"; "There are six days of creation"; "There are seven deadly sins"), as it is an almost wildly unmanageable collection of declarations ("God was in Christ reconciling the world"; "Forgive them for they know not what they do"; "Neither do I condemn you; go, and sin no more"). To be sure, one has to reflect systematically on the meanings explicit or implicit in such declarations, and that is what certain kinds of professional theologians do. But since the declarations confront us with the aura of mystery—in the above instances the mystery of a reconciling, forgiving God—our dissection of them must always be tentative, since no finite human mind, or combination of finite human minds, can exhaust the meaning of the mystery. Every human perception will be no more than partial. Intellectual modesty is the hallmark of an authentic theologian.

This is where the love letter comes in, for a love letter is also always skirting the edge of mystery. We can love someone for twenty years and be provided with a fixed and sure center and core of our being. But when we come to express all that in a letter to the one we love, the ways in which we express it will change tremendously over the twenty-year span. The first gushing and excited letters, early in a courtship, will not be disavowed by the writer two decades later, when they are discovered in a long-forgotten box in the attic. But in the intervening years the relationship will have matured in so many ways that a markedly different tone will be present in the recent letters, reflecting, perhaps, how their love survived some very stormy periods, how their relationship helped them cope with the death of a child, how their delight in little things like shared glances or gestures has not only persisted but deepened in the interval.

The love endures, the means for expressing the love change. So to say that theology is a love letter to God and to the church and to the people, is a way of saying that the very fact that the love endures means that the ways of expressing it will change.

No theology is eternal. Indeed, it is a sign of vitality and growth when new theologies, such as liberation theology, appear on the scene, so long as it is always remembered that their love letter, too, is never more than a pale reflection of the real thing.

Theology as the "Second Act"

What appears to come first actually comes second. Theology is not the first thing that Christians "do." The first thing (as we saw in chapter 1) is *compromiso*, commitment. Following that, and growing out of it is theology, which, as Gutiérrez puts it, is always "the second act."

It makes all the difference in the world to what (or to whom) we are initially committed. If we are committed as U.S. citizens to "staying Number One at all costs," our resultant "theology" will justify waging war in order to maintain that position, exploiting the poor in order to have more for ourselves, and passing punitive measures against the poor or the homeless or the destitute or the dark-skinned, in case they begin to threaten the security and survival of our "commitment." In addition, it is easy to cheat on the evidence, so that we will not have to second-guess the appropriateness of our initial commitment. We are extraordinarily adept at what is called "rationalizing," finding reasons *after* the fact to justify what we have already done and want to continue doing.

Liberation theologians, however, are not talking about

just any old sort of commitment. They are talking about *commitment to the poor*, by which they mean taking sides with the poor in their struggle to escape from poverty and attain human dignity. This is particularly threatening to the readers (and the writer) of this book, since we are not for the most part poor, and we realize immediately that if more is given to the poor there will be less for us. (We will pursue this dilemma in chapter 5, especially pp. 95–98.)

The commitment being described is not a form of intellectualizing so much as one of experiencing and "encountering" (the word in the chapter title is very important). It is not enough to read books about poverty; commitment means encountering poor people. It is not enough to learn about "the root causes of poverty," though that is obviously important; it is a matter of learning about, and entering into, and making common cause with, persons who are being destroyed by those root causes, and seeking for legislative—or more drastic—ways to dispose of the causes. And it is the almost universal witness of those who do so, that in encountering the poor they are somehow encountering God, learning that whoever else God is, God is "the God of the poor," the one who takes their part, who works with and for them. This is what "a preferential option for the poor" is all about.

Those who are living in the midst of such a situation *do* engage in "the second act," the attempt to think through, in the light of faith, what this all means for them and what it demands of them.

This approach is not actually as avant-garde as it may appear, though its earlier reality has been obscured for hundreds of years. One of the basic patterns in medieval thought, for example, was propounded by Saint Anselm: "I believe in order that I may understand." To "believe" something is to be committed to it, to make a venture of faith before all the evidence is in, to risk that it is right and true. To "understand" something is to reflect on the belief, to think through its implications and what it calls on us to do. And that is what we have already identified as "the second act." To be sure, we must not press the comparison too far; Anselm's encounter was in a chapel, and Gutiérrez's encounter was in a barrio. But each encounter provides material for "the second act."

A further by-product of this interplay is that it rules out static and "fixed" positions, just as the love letter does. We do not get locked into a view of God, partial at best, that is unyielding, nor can we ever rest content that finally we have learned all there is to know about God. Whatever else God is, God is mystery, and our human penetrations of that mystery will always be, and always *must* be, tentative and exploratory, subject to never-ending refinement.

Critical Reflection on Praxis
in the Light of the Word of God

We have been virtually tripping over another way of stating what liberation theology is all about, a formal (and formidable) definition that casts more light on our inquiry. Theology is "critical reflection on praxis in the light of the Word of God." If we break that statement down into its component parts it is not so threatening. Let us begin with the least familiar word, *praxis*.

Praxis is not quite the same as "practice." To speak of "a praxis situation" is to describe the tension between *reflection* and *action*. It is a situation in which we are always involved, whether we are aware of it or not. Descriptively, we can start either way: "We reflect, and on the basis of that reflection, we act," or, "We act, and in the light of that action we reflect on what we have done." What matters is that we are always living in the midst of both, in a never-ending process. On the basis of that original action, we reflect again on where it has gotten us, and on the basis of that new reflection we act again, but in a different way.

On and on and on.

The back-and-forth flow never ceases. Suppose we act unwisely. Then we reflect on what went wrong, and try to devise an action that will bring us the hoped-for results. We will never exhaust this process and arrive at full wisdom and totally correct actions. (The people in the world to fear the most are those who claim that they *have* put it all together and know exactly what they—and we—must do.)

But theology is not just reflection and action. Christians are to engage in *"critical* reflection and action," using their minds to the utmost in seeking better solutions to problems, and assessing both reflection and action to determine whether they were wise or foolish, ingenious or stupid, timid or rash. "Critical reflection and action" is a troubling exercise because often (probably more often than not) we have to make negative judgments about our past reflections and actions, and that is an exercise we would just as soon forego.

But liberation theologians offer some help in coping with that. For there is a criterion they bring to bear on reflection and action. Some people engage in "critical reflection on praxis in the light of . . ." the Marxist dialectic, or the Seven-Fold Path of Enlightenment, or rigidly controlled empirical data, or glorified hunches about what "feels good." By contrast, liberation theologians offer a different criterion: they engage in "critical reflection on praxis *in the light of the Word of God.*" That is clearly a criterion and a demanding one, but on first acquaintance it seems to raise as many questions as it solves. For, to join the issue bluntly, how can we know what the "Word of God" *is?*

There are at least four responses to the question, and whatever "answer" there is will involve ongoing interplay between them all.

First, the basic meaning of "the Word of God" for Christians is *Jesus Christ.* The word *Word* (*dabar* in Hebrew, *logos* in Greek) has meanings both clear and subtle. The prologue to the Fourth Gospel, after describing the Word of God as the creative power of God that brought the world into being and sustains it, goes on to say that the same Word was "made flesh," given embodiment in a human life, in Jesus of Nazareth. The Word of God, then, is present in our midst, as one of us, in the person of a first-century Jewish rabbi who provides us, in a fully human life, with the best clues we have about God.

Second, the *Bible,* the Jewish and Christian scriptures, provides a written account of the story of Jesus as the embodiment of the creative power of God, "pitching his tent" in our midst. This has led many Christians to call the Bible itself the Word of God, but this short-circuits the process, confusing the witness and the one to whom the witness points. The Bible is our best (and only available) witness to the story of "the Word of God . . . made flesh," a story we cannot learn elsewhere. So the Bible is crucial to our understanding.

Third, Catholic Christianity more than Protestant Christianity has appealed to *tradition* as a further source in understanding the Word of God with which scripture confronts us. The Latin word *traditio* means "that which is handed on." There have been twenty centuries since the Word made flesh walked the earth, and it has been almost that long since accounts of his life were made available in written form. That is a long gap, and in the intervening centuries "tradition" has tried to "hand on" interpretations of the story. As a result, we do not have to reinvent the wheel every time we reflect about the Word of God. People have been doing it for two thousand years. As John Robertson said to the Pilgrims when they embarked for the new world, "God has yet more light to break forth from his Holy Word." Tradition is the way fresh truth and understanding are incorporated into the story.

To be sure, tradition can become the dead hand of the past on the present, but it can also be energizing and liberating, providing help in thinking through what the faith must mean today, and not just what it meant yesterday.

Finally, *the human conscience* is a clue to the Word of God. Sometimes Jesus' message is manipulated; sometimes the biblical message is misunderstood; sometimes tradition goes askew. At such times, the power of the human conscience helps to sort things out. The institution of slavery, for example, has been "justified" in the Christian tradition by using carefully selected biblical verses, or manipulating Jesus' or Paul's words about "servants." When this happens, sooner or later individuals and groups rise up, pit their consciences against such distortions, and help to set the church on a new track, nourished out of their own exposure to the Word of God in ways that are not self-serving.

This is precisely what has been going on in the development of liberation theology. For centuries, the Christian message was tamed: "Servants obey your masters"; "The poor you have always with you"; "Let women keep silence in church." And it is through fresh encounters with the Word of God in the person of Jesus Christ, and the message of scripture, that we are beginning to understand Christ in a new way (which is really a rediscovery of an "old" way), hear messages from the Bible that were camouflaged for centuries, and unravel traditions that became the property of vested interests using the Word of God for their own ends.

"Critical reflection on praxis in the light of the Word of God" is our best safeguard against the gospel being derailed again. And if, nonetheless, that happens, the same process of self-correction will finally prevail once again.

The Good News of Liberation

The central message of liberation theology is, not surprisingly, the good news of liberation. The *content* of the good news of liberation is, somewhat surprisingly, threefold.[3] The three emphases cannot be separated. If we try to do so, we miss the point and falsify. Each emphasis must include the other two. No exceptions. (It is important to remember this in the following paragraphs, where, bound by the rules of linguistic discourse, we can only talk about one thing at a time.)

The *first* emphasis in liberation theology is *liberation from unjust social structures* that destroy people. The structures may be political or economic or cultural; they may grow out of warped attitudes based on race, class, nation, or sex; they may also, sad to relate, be embodied in ecclesiastical structures as well, providing religious sanctions for evil. Liberation theologians have emphasized this dimension of "structural evil," since it is the most immediate barrier to full personhood in the lives of the poor. Doing so has thrust many of them into conflictive situations and accounts for many of the murders that are a part of Latin American church life.

The liberation message on this first level is the invitation to work for change, for reform, or, if necessary, for the destruction of social structures that are evil rather than good.

The *second* emphasis in liberation theology is more subtle but equally devastating. It is *liberation from the power of fate*, from the sense that one's station in life is foreordained, and that not only is there nothing one can do about it, but that it would be presumptuous and arrogant even to try. If one is born poor, that is the way it was meant to be; if one is born rich, that, too, is the way it was meant to be—all of which translates into good news to the rich and bad news to the poor. This appeal to fate leads to apathy or despair among the poor, and exhilaration among the rich, who, quite understandably, are determined to keep things that way.

(For hundreds of years the churches played a major role in supporting this position by the simple device of substituting "providence" or "the will of God" for the pagan concept of "fate." Accept your lot without complaint, the sermons went, since that is God's will for you, and if you live without complaint God will reward you in the afterlife.)

The liberation message on this second level is that things need *not* remain the way they are, for the biblical God is working actively for justice and seeks to enlist all of God's people in the struggle. The operative word is hope.

The *third* emphasis in liberation theology is *liberation*

from personal sin and guilt. This is not an addition to the original liberation agenda, inserted late in the day to forestall the critics. It has been there from the start. If it receives less quantitative treatment than the other two, this is for the very good reason that it has *always* been the central (if not exclusive) message of the institutional church, hardly in need of new champions, whereas the first two emphases have only infrequently been acknowledged in the past as valid parts of the Christian agenda.

The liberation message on this third level is the reality of gratuitousness of grace—the assurance that the resources of divine mercy and forgiveness are always at hand, gifts ready to be bestowed on all who ask for them.

Let us repeat the warning at the beginning of this section: we are not understanding liberation theology correctly as long as we are aware of only one, or only two, of these three emphases. All three must be present. No reductionism. The point must be stressed because those who are critical of liberation theology usually assert, incorrectly, that it is concerned exclusively with the first emphasis and never talks about the third. Not so.

Jesus as Liberator

We must personalize the quality of liberation more than the previous discussion suggests. We can do this by affirming the specifically Christian claim of Jesus as Liberator. There have been many names and titles for Jesus of Nazareth: Lord, Messiah, Master, Son of God, Son of Man, Teacher, Victor, Lamb of God, Healer, Savior, and (as we have just seen) Word. No single title by itself suffices, and even if they were taken together, the result would be less than the sum of its parts. In liberation theology, the claim that Jesus is the liberator—the one who sets free, the one who empowers, the one who makes all things new—is, after long neglect in Christian history, being appreciated again. Jesus is seen by eyes of faith as the personalized presence and power of God in each of the three liberation emphases we have just explored. He liberates from the destructiveness of social structures by offering himself as a focal point of commitment more enduring and fulfilling than commitment to any social structure could ever be; he liberates from fate by demonstrating that new things are always possible, and that the dignity of human choice is not to be surrendered but to be enhanced; and he liberates from personal sin and guilt by the nature of his forgiving love, a love channeled through him by God.

He also liberates us from time-worn images that do not speak to our day. What is so fresh in the approach of liberation theology is that it offers a better "handle" on the meaning of Jesus than many varieties of contemporary theology. The great problem with conventional theology has been that it *begins* its presentation of Jesus with the *conclusion* reached by the early church. By the fourth century Christians were affirming Christ as a divine being, the Lord of heaven, sitting on a throne, far removed from the human scene. So exalted and remote did he become that his role as mediator between God and humanity was almost superseded by the role assigned to Mary, who was increasingly looked upon as a mediator between *Christ* and humanity, since no one could get near such an exalted Christ without her help. This whole approach has been known as *Christology from above*.

Liberation theology, by contrast, has followed the route of *Christology from below*. It starts where the first disciples started and retraces the route they walked, knowing Jesus initially as a first-century Jew, a rabbi (or teacher) with special communication skills, a compassionate and loving person who welcomed women and children into places previously reserved for men alone, one in whose presence people felt strengthened and affirmed . . . and one who also judged, when occasion called for it. He shared bread with his friends, got hungry as they did, and experienced fatigue, discouragement, and pain. This relationship was brutally severed by his death, and for a while it seemed as though they had lost him. But they came to believe that he had not left them, save physically, and that the powers of death had been unable to destroy him.

At first they tried to describe him with familiar human labels: teacher, friend, counselor, healer. But these increasingly proved inadequate. And so titles redolent of divinity as well as humanity were attached to his name, culminating finally in a recognition of both his humanity and his divinity, even though they did not have a vocabulary that did justice to such a monumental claim.

This second route to an understanding of Jesus has been of central importance in Latin America because, as we have seen, to affirm the presence of Jesus "in the midst" is simultaneously to affirm the presence of *God* "in the midst" as well. That God is the "God of life," not death, the God who is found not only in the great cathedrals at the time of the elevation of the Host, but the God who has shared the human lot of suffering, hunger, disappointment, torture, death—and resurrection. If Christ is present with them, right where they are, they feel empowered to struggle and work and pray and plant and hoe and have dreams for their children. They have been liberated from their despair and hopelessness, and that is good news indeed.

It is important to note that Mary too has a new and special role in Latin American Christianity, not as the quasi-deified being in holy pictures who is totally removed from earth and earthiness, but as a peasant woman, much like peasant women today, who was poor and uneducated and probably had no more than one pair of shoes, and yet through whom Jesus of Nazareth was born. She sings of justice, of the overthrow of the mighty, of food for the hungry, of support for the needy, and when she appears in a vision at Guadalupe she is not a Spanish lady of high nobility, but a humble Amerindian woman. That, also, is good news indeed.

To Know God Is to Do Justice

Our survey will be both incomplete and misleading unless we underline the fact that theology and ethics can never be separated in liberation thought. This can be confirmed by brief attention to one of the most widely used biblical passages in Latin America, Jeremiah 22:13–17, the theme of which is that "to know God is to do justice."

The prophet Jeremiah is engaging in a favorite indoor sport of prophets, king-bashing. The king is trying to project a royal image by building a palace he doesn't need, garish beyond description and constructed of the most expensive building materials available by a group of laborers who are not getting a cent for their work. Jehoiakim is trying to show who's really in charge.

Jeremiah is not impressed. He taunts the king by comparing him to his father, king before him, a type of put-down no grown man needs. "Your father," Jeremiah thunders in judgmental tones, "dealt justly and fairly," and he "upheld the cause of the lowly and poor." The contrasts between the two kings are already plain to see. And then comes the rhetorical question: "Is this not what it means to know me?" asks God. And Jeremiah and Jehoiakim both know that the answer can only be yes. What it means to know God *is* to "deal justly and fairly," and to "uphold the cause of the lowly and poor." Conversely, what it means *not* to know God is to deal *un*justly and crookedly, to demean the cause of the lowly and poor, by (to take the nearest example at hand) making men work without pay or health benefits on an unneeded palace.

One can affirm God with all the right words, have an impeccable theology (even one called "liberation theology"), and put money in the collection plate—and yet if one is not "doing justice," the words are hollow, the faith is spurious, the gestures are meaningless, and the religious stance being displayed is really atheism. "To know God is to do justice." No separation of the two is possible.

There is a prayer some people pray without admitting it, a prayer that a few other people are honest enough to acknowledge is what they really desire.

It goes, "Our Father who art in heaven . . . stay there!"

We can cope with a God who is sequestered in some corner of heaven (or even center stage), but *far off*—which is where we like our gods to be—safely removed from our dwelling place and therefore no threat to us.

Liberation theology is about the God who refuses to answer that prayer.[4]

4

A New Way of Being the Church

(the genie that won't go back in the bottle)

> If they ever take our radio, suspend our newspapers,
> silence us, put to death all our priests, bishops
> included, and you are left alone—a people without
> priests—then each of you will have to be God's
> microphone. Each of you will have to be a messenger,
> a prophet. The church will always exist as long as even
> one baptized person is left alive.
>
> —Archbishop Romero

In the summer of 1988, a week-long birthday celebration for Gustavo Gutiérrez was held at Maryknoll, New York.[1] Not untypically, he had to miss part of it, having earlier agreed to speak to the Anglican bishops at Lambeth in England. The midweek trip involved two overnight flights, irregular meals, and a six-hour time zone change—all staples in the life of the brand new sexagenarian. But in addition to its outward trappings, the trip produced one imperishable bit of comparative ecclesiology. Reflecting after his return about differences between Roman Catholic and Anglican churches, Gutiérrez said, "In Roman Catholicism, we have many rules; is very difficult. It seems to me that in Anglicanism there are many customs; is more difficult."

The Discovery of the Future—A Look at the Past

The church did not suddenly spring into existence within living memory. It has been around a long, long

time—long enough to accumulate both rules and customs. We need to know just a bit about its past if we are to
understand its present and think about its future.[2]

We have already noted the mixed message that accom-
panied the transplanting of the church from Europe to
Latin America in the fifteenth century, symbolized by the
different approaches of Christopher Columbus and Bartolomé de las Casas. For Columbus, and especially for his
ideological descendants, the church came to Latin America with all the trappings of European power, a partner
(whether willing or not) in the domination of the Indians,
part of a system that condoned pillage, rape, torture,
slavery, exploitation, and forced conversions, all to satisfy
the conquistadors' greed for gold. For Las Casas, on the
other hand, the Indians were to be treated as fully human
persons, invited but not coerced into accepting Christianity, allowed to live their lives in the way they chose, free
of white domination.

The way of Columbus set the pattern, however, and
even though some of the original excesses were later
contained, the church remained hand in glove with the
explorers, its leadership securely in the hands of the
Spaniards. With the passage of time, the overt political
control of Europe over the Latin American colonies was
diminished, but the covert economic control was retained
and, in a descriptive adage repeated generation after
generation, "the rich get richer while the poor become
poorer."

The *old* "way of being the church" was to accept all
this.

Whatever prevailed on the economic front—massive
wealth for a few, grinding poverty for all the rest—was to
be understood as God's design. The resultant message

was clear: accept your lot, whether good or bad, don't make waves, and you will receive a reward in heaven. This was a splendid agenda for the rich, but hardly good news for the poor.

But there gradually began to be stirrings that this goal of acceptance of the way things are was something less than the full message of liberation that the Hebrew prophets and Jesus and occasional later brave men and women had preached and lived and died for. We have examined some of these stirrings in earlier chapters: a conviction that "the world should not be the way it is," a rediscovery of the biblical notion of "the preferential option for the poor," a new accent on hope, and a recognition of the possibility of liberation from oppressive social structures and the iron-clad rule of fate.

A new way of being the church began to emerge, a way that approached the future with openness and hope—a belief that change was mandated by the gospel, that God wills more than destitution for the human family, and that those within the church could, and should, be enlisted in the process of transformation not only of individuals but of social structures as well.

This new hope for the future began at the grass roots, in the emergence of what were called "base communities," at which we shall presently look. But before doing so, we must note a few events that gave support to the beginnings of "a new way of being the church." Prominent were conferences of Catholic bishops in Latin America, held at Medellín, Colombia, in 1968, and in Puebla, Mexico, in 1975.[3] The impetus for these conferences came in turn from the Second Vatican Council, held in Rome in the years 1962–1965, and comprised of the leadership of the entire Catholic world. Among the achievements of the

Council, one is particularly important for the concerns of this chapter. This was a new approach to the understanding of the church. The old view said in effect, the church is basically the hierarchy, the governing leadership, who stand above the laity; lay persons accept the decisions of the hierarchy. The new view, which prevailed, said in effect, the church is basically "the people of God," the *whole* people of God, most of whom are lay folks, out of which some can be called to positions of authority and leadership.

The Vatican Council went on to reassert many ways in which the church must involve itself in the affairs of the world, with concern not only about heaven but about earth as well, and concern for what happens to people on earth—everything from support for labor unions, fair wages, and the right to strike, to condemnation of indiscriminate bombing of civilians in time of war.

The conference at Medellín rode in on the wave of these emphases. Its method was to examine the nature of society sociologically, reflect on what it discovered theologically, and then offer specific proposals for transformation. The sociological starting point was itself a breakthrough and meant that old bromides had to be discarded and new realities accepted, such as the ongoing reality of violence in unjust social structures even if no overt physical destruction was going on; an acknowledgment of "class tensions," not as a Marxist import but as a sheer description of the social reality; a recognition that peace must be linked to justice if it is not to be indulgent; and a need for the church to defend the rights of the oppressed, adopt a simpler life-style, and so on. Without using the exact words, Medellín also affirmed a "preferential option for the poor" as a mandate to the church and to society as a whole, and gave new space for the role laity could play in the life of the church.

The years after Medellín were not serene, and we will look at some of the conflicts later in this chapter. On one hand, back in their own dioceses after Medellín's adjournment, conservative bishops set themselves against implementing the guidelines they had so recently approved. Lay people, on the other hand, interpreted Medellín as building on Vatican II, acknowledging that the laity were to be active, policy-setting members rather than only passive recipients of the sacraments. Liberation theology, hovering on the edges of its initial articulation, burst forth in full bloom almost coincident with the Medellín conference, and the base communities swept like a prairie fire across the ecclesiastically parched terrain.

The conference at Puebla, eleven years later, did not produce much that was brand new, but it played the inestimably vital role of preserving the breakthroughs of Medellín—especially in relation to the base communities, liberation theology, and responsible roles for the laity— against fruitless conservative attempts to put the genie back in the bottle. If Medellín guaranteed the genie's exit, Puebla offered assurances that there would be no return to its previous confinement.

The Discovery of One Another—The Base Communities

Perhaps the most important thing to say initially about the base communities is what they are not. They are *not* "rival churches" or "parallel churches" trying to woo cradle Catholics away from the spiritual home of their upbringing and into some kind of sect. Those who are

members of base communities have not "left the church."
They are simply participating in "a new way of being the
church" and are often also involved in the life of the large
building on the town square. But in ways no one could
have foreseen, even two decades ago, they have become
part of an exciting movement whose reality they can only
attribute to the activity of the Holy Spirit.

What, then, *are* the base communities? They are small
groups of Christians, perhaps fifteen to thirty people, who
get together about once a week. They discuss local problems and what to do about them, such as the polluted water
supply, the unnecessary brutality of the police chief toward
their sons and daughters, the need to stand together in the
face of a new land tax. They study scripture (as we will see
later), they sing, they pray with and for one another, and
they may have a Eucharist if a priest is present. They
designedly do not have a national organization or "head-
quarters," being very anxious not to get overorganized and
lose their sense of immediacy on the local scene.

There may be as many as one hundred thousand such
communities throughout Latin America, with at least
eighty thousand in Brazil alone, though nobody has an
exact head count and few people actually care about the
numbers game. (As Gustavo Gutiérrez comments, "When
we say 'eighty thousand,' or 'one hundred thousand,' what
we really mean is 'many, many communities.' ")

The communities clearly fill a need that can be filled in
no other way. A church in a rural area or an urban barrio
may have one priest to minister to three or four thousand
communicants. This is hardly the stuff of intimate community building. And so individuals find one another,
share their sense of isolation and need for empowerment,
begin to get together informally, and then more formally

and regularly; and almost before one notices, the assorted individuals have become a "community"—still members of a huge parish church but also members of a small, intimate, and life-giving reality.

A North American observer might be inclined to think, "It sounds just like an active Bible study group in one of our churches." That might not be too far off the mark, save that the dynamic in Latin America comes quite literally "from the base," that is, from the poor who are at the bottom (or the "base") of society, so that the intensity and the need and the importance of staying together is considerably stronger than what one may find in a middle-class church in the heartland of America.

There is no overall descriptive device that covers the full nature of the base communities, since each one is trying to respond to its own unique situation, replicable nowhere else. This means that all generalizations about them are dangerous and to some degree inaccurate. Nevertheless we can fill out our brief picture with the help of Guillermo Cook, who has done extensive study of the base communities and finds the following five characteristics to be widespread:

The base communities clearly emphasize the *centrality of the gospel*. Their study of scripture, their enactment of liturgy, distinguishes them from many other "action groups."

They all make *an option for the poor*. This is not surprising, since the huge majority of them *are* poor and have made the exciting discovery that God cares even for them and offers salvation even to them.

There is a stress on *liberation and conscientization*. Members of the communities are *working* for justice (liberation) and *educating* for justice (conscientization).

They have *"a missionary approach to ecclesiastical struc-tures."* They see "structures" in the church as necessary but not sacrosanct. Some structures endure (the Eucharist remains central); others are expendable (the mass is no longer said in Latin). The communities therefore have the flexibility to respond to fresh needs as they arrive.

They practice *respect for others,* even those to whom they are opposed.[4]

There is a saying in Latin America that whereas most people experience oppression, women are *triply* op-pressed: they are poor, they are women, and they are Catholic. Socioeconomic oppression is the lot of most of the poor, and women are no exception; gender oppres-sion is almost universal in the *macho* culture of Latin America, where women are often seen simply as sex objects and denied any real power in their own lives or the life of their nation. Religious oppression is similarly wide-spread in a patriarchal church that *de jure* denies women the right to ordained leadership, and *de facto* denies them any significant roles in church leadership. What is true of the rest of the culture is usually true in the church as well: men run the show and women sit on the sidelines.

With one significant exception . . .

It is women who for the most part have brought the base communities into being and keep them going. They have refused in the base communities to accept the sec-ond- or third-class citizenship the church imposes on them elsewhere. Gustavo Gutiérrez has acknowledged that he cannot conceive of the extraordinary impact of the base communities apart from the initial and ongoing im-pact of the women upon them. They may be denied holy orders, but they live holy lives.

A twofold process is at work: they strengthen the base

communities and the base communities strengthen them. I can best illustrate this by sharing two visits my wife and I had in Ocotal, the town in Nicaragua near the Honduran border that was the object of frequent border raids, one of which was described in the Introduction to this volume.

One afternoon we met with four women who were discouraged, dejected, and defeated. They shared a common reason for their mood: each had had a teenage son kidnapped by contra troops who came over the border from Honduras, snatched these and other young men, took them back to Honduras where they were trained against their will in the art of guerrilla warfare, so that in the future they could return as part of guerrilla units and, if necessary, fire on their own families. From previous experience, the women knew that this was happening, and they were powerless to do anything about it. They pleaded with us, in the midst of tears, to carry their concerns back to U.S. officials and thus bring about the release of their sons, since they knew full well that the contras were dependent on U.S. military aid to carry out their activities. The tone of the meeting was one of utter sadness, for, knowing the deafness of the Reagan administration to such pleas, we could make no promises, and they recognized that their request was a long shot at best.

About two hours after that meeting we were invited to another meeting, this time of the base community in Ocotal. It was the day before Palm Sunday. Palm Sunday was going to be a big day in Ocotal—as it is throughout Latin America—and a life-sized statue of Christ on a donkey had been created, in front of which palm leaves were going to be strewn all the way to the cathedral. And what absolutely blew our minds as gringo spectators was that the people who ran that base community meeting,

concerned both with parade logistics and an extended
Bible study of the triumphal entry, were the same four
women with whom we had earlier talked. But now, rather
than tears, there was purpose, direction, resolve. They
were empowered. They shared the joy of the base community at the thought of what was going to happen: Jesus
was going to come into Ocotal the next day and be ac-
claimed by the multitudes. They knew, of course, that the
acclaim was not going to last, and that a long and bloody
week lay ahead before the final triumph of Easter, but
they entered into the joyous mood of the "Hosannas" of
the crowd of people welcoming Jesus. It was clear that
their strength came because the base community was
continuing to sustain them, just as it was sustaining all
the other people in that little village up by the border,
consisting of their friends and relatives who also had
family members who had been raped, tortured, murdered, or abducted. And yet, within the structure of that
base community they could find ways to rejoice and look
forward in hope to the promise that things can really
change.

The Discovery of the Bible—A Charter for Change

Recall the episode in chapter 2. Bartolomé de las Casas
is getting ready to preach. He searches for a text. He finds
one, and then devoutly wishes he had not. For rather than
leaving him awash with eternal verities, it challenges him
to the core. If the text is right, his life is wrong; if the text is
true, his life is false; if the text is God's Word, he has some
serious business to attend to with the Almighty; if the text
makes demands, he has no choice but to obey.

The experience of Las Casas is not unique. Throughout

Christian history there have been similar dramatic encounters between individuals and God—Augustine, Mar-
tin Luther, and John Wesley immediately come to mind—
who discovered that the printed words upon a page were
not lifeless smudges, but living exhortations, assurances,
challenges, and empowerments, communicating something of crucial importance from God to the reader.

But until recently, there have not been many repeti-
tions of the Las Casas experience in Latin America, for the
simple reason that as "culture Catholicism" developed in
the centuries after Las Casas died, the Bible ceased to play
an important role in the life of Christians. For one thing,
only a minority of the people could read; for another,
those who had a "religious book" would be much more
likely to have a missal, containing the full text of the mass
and other liturgical exercises that guided their lives. If a
Christian had questions or perplexities, it was not necessary to wrestle with a strange book, for Father was always
on hand and Father knew all the answers.

But, as we have seen in the above pages, all this has
begun to change. For the power of the base communities
is not just the power of brave and dedicated people; it is
the power of those same people seeking to discern God's
will for them, and turning to scripture as an important
source of insight. Unlike Las Casas, who made his discovery alone, they struggle with the Bible in community. And
their recent access to the texts of scripture has been a
crucial event in their own story of empowerment.

Gustavo Gutiérrez, who has participated in many such
base community gatherings, says that communities must
approach the Bible "in an attitude of faith." There is a
dialogue "between faith and faith," between the believers
of the past and the believers of today. The Bible tells us

stories about people who lived in past time, and we who
live in the present time supply a connection, for we read
their stories in the light of our stories. "When a passage is
read," Gutiérrez reports, "it is not unusual for someone
to say, for example, 'That is what happened to me a short
time ago.' "[5] And that is when the real "conversation"
with the Bible begins. There is *nearness* of an unexpected
kind because of the similarity of stories. And at the same
time, there is a *distance* that must be honored. We must
not try to make "them" contemporaries of ours, nor pre-
tend that we can be "ancients" with them. But with an
acknowledgment of both nearness and distance, new insights can come. This is part of what Gutiérrez means
when he says that not only do we read the text, "but the
text reads us."

Those who live in such situations do not have the
advantage of sophisticated commentaries, or knowledge
of the original Hebrew and Greek, although sometimes a
priest can supply such background. The real dynamic
comes from the people themselves, many of whom cannot read or write, but whose insights are often breathtak-
ingly appropriate—in part, perhaps, because they are
precisely the sort of people for whom the scriptures were
originally written.

There can be a mature naïveté that gets to the heart of
the matter. On one occasion, while their own bishop,
Dom Pedro Casaldáliga, was under house arrest, a base
community in Brazil was studying the passage in Acts
12:1–17, in which Peter is freed from prison by an angel.
This is the stuff for which practices like "demythologization" were created. But a woman in the group (who, we
may be sure, had never heard of "demythologization"),
found the perfect contemporary analogy to relate the

ancient text to the present situation and give them both new life:

> When Dom Pedro Casaldáliga was a prisoner in his house, no one knew. There was no means of communication. Seven well-armed police officers kept watch at the house and refused to let anyone enter or leave. Exactly like Peter's prison in the Bible. But a young girl went in. No one took any notice of her. She was an ordinary girl, in cheap flip-flops. She took a note from Dom Pedro out of his prison, went straight to the airstrip, got a lift to Goiânia, and told the bishops who were meeting there. They got busy and got Dom Pedro freed. The girl was the angel of God who made the gates of Peter's prison swing open.[6]

Frei Betto, a Dominican priest from Brazil, offers an arresting contrast between the way "traditional priests" and members of the base communities use scripture. It is close enough to the mark to apply to the rest of us as well. We tend to use the Bible as a *window*, enabling us to see what is happening somewhere else—"Bible times," for example, when God was fairly available—and we hope to be transformed by what we see out there. Members of the base communities, by contrast, use the Bible as a *mirror*, in which they see their own reality reflected and hope to learn about themselves in the process. "The people feel as though they are seeing their own lives revealed in the accounts of the Bible." Frei Betto proposes that we sophisticated ones return "the keys of the Bible" to the people since they are using it so creatively.

Actual Bible study is probably less sharply divided than the example suggests, and at its best there are elements of both window and mirror in scriptural appropriation. Scholars talk about a "circulation" in interpreting the Bible. We bring our experience *to* the Bible, we draw new insight *from* the Bible, we go back to our own situation *with* the Bible, and see it all in a new way. *This process is never completed.* Each "circulation" helps us to reflect and act, act and reflect, more creatively.

Carlos Mesters, a Dutch priest who has worked with base communities for twenty years in Brazil, summarizes his own experience:

> They do not stop at the text-in-itself or the facts related by the text, but these become a base and a starting-point for discovering a deeper meaning which has to do with their own lives and the situation in which they live. . . . Biblical history, without ceasing to be history, becomes a symbol or a *mirror* of the present situation as the people experience it in their community. Life and Bible mix. There is both mutual interference and illumination. (italics mine)[7]

Much is made in liberation theology of the phrase "a militant reading of scripture." Sometimes the phrase simply refers to the aggressive tone of the exegete, but more often it describes the *content* of the biblical message itself, with its challenges to the established order and its proposals for a new society. There are a host of such passages, particularly in the Hebrew prophets, but elsewhere as well, where a stern and devastating word from on high is spoken about the inadequacy and injustice of many of our human arrangements that enable a few to prosper to an obscene degree at the cost of gouging and destroying the many. (Let those who are sceptical turn to such passages as the Exodus story, 2 Samuel 11:2–12:7; Jeremiah 22:13–17; Daniel 3; Luke 1:46–55; Matthew 25:31–46, and almost at random in the prophets.) Those are easy-to-find illustrations.

But the theme is present not only in stern or apocalyp-

tic passages but throughout scripture in places we least
expect it. A convenient example of the disarming power
of scripture is Gutiérrez's treatment of the biblical image
of "the temple"—an innocent enough topic, seemingly
devoid of "militancy."[8] In the Hebrew scriptures there are
various acknowledgments of sacred space. Sinai is a sacred *mountain,* abode of an awesome deity who occasionally makes more localized appearances to wandering
tribesmen in a *tent,* and then, more substantially in an *ark*
that can be carried from place to place—even into battle—
and that represents God's ongoing presence. After the
people establish a permanent dwelling place, the presence of God is established in the *temple* in Jerusalem,
containing a "holy of holies" where the ark is permanently lodged.

In the Christian scriptures, the understanding of the
temple moves in unexpected new directions. The clear
presence of the divine is represented in the person of
Christ, the temple imagery is consciously adopted in
speaking of him: "Destroy this temple," Jesus says in the
Fourth Gospel, "and I will raise it again," after which (so
that we will not miss the point) the author explains that
"the temple he was speaking of was his body." The
"space" where God is especially present in human life is
no longer an immobile building but a very mobile human
being: *Christ is the temple of God.*

Paul goes further. He develops the image of the Christian community as itself a "temple" of living stones. "The
temple of God," he asserts unambiguously, "is holy, and
that temple you are." Not only is Christ the temple of
God; *every Christian is the temple of God.*

Even that is not the end of the story. In the early church
the gift of the Holy Spirit is poured out on Gentiles as well

as Jews; *all* can become the "place" where God dwells. The authority of Jesus is cited once again: "Anyone who loves me will heed what I say; then God will love that one, and we will come and make our dwelling place within that one." Humanity itself has become the "temple," the "space" wherein God is clearly found: *every person is the temple of God*.

What is so "militant" about this? To build "the temple of God" is to invest all one's energies in the well-being of *every member* of the human family without exception— single parents, Sandinistas, gays/lesbians/straights, corporation executives, unemployed machinists. If any of them have too much—or too little—the task is to work for rearrangement of whatever forces in society produce that distortion of what God intends. If any child is hungry, rearrangement of the economy is called for. If billions go to armaments that will destroy even a single "temple of God," national priorities are to be rearranged. If a single person is tortured, rearrangement of the laws that permit it must be invoked. If a single person is unemployed or homeless, rearrangements of the allocation of goods and resources belong at the top of human concerns. And if rearrangement is not enough? Then the Bible cries out that more radical means are called for; overthrowing existing structures of injustice and replacing them with new ones that foster justice.

The agenda is ample enough for many lifetimes.

The Discovery of Conflict—A Look at the Structures

Earlier we referred to conflicts that emerged after Medellín and Puebla, and they are a part of the story, even though it is not necessary to develop them in detail.

It is almost enough to remark that *any* attempts at change in *any* institution at *any* time in history will encounter rough waters. (No one who has ever tried to change a time-honored custom in a local church will have difficulty believing this.) The post–Vatican II years, and the post–Medellín/Puebla years have been no exception to the rule.[9]

The chief charge laid at the door of liberation theologians has been that they are Marxists. The charge need not be refuted in detail because all attempts (even official ones) to sustain the charge have been unavailing. Gustavo Gutiérrez has been the chief target of this attack, and his replies, along with the patent depth of his Christian insight and commitment, and along with his biblically oriented theology, provide ample refutation to all but the most hardened critics.

I believe that the real "problem" liberation theology raises for its critics is its radically biblical character. Catholic critics are not used to according the Bible the central place it has in Gutiérrez's thought, and they sometimes feel that he does not give corresponding attention to tradition, the other pole of Catholic theology. Protestant critics, usually inured to the idea of the Bible as a charter for radical change, are rendered uncomfortable by the biblical perspective Gutiérrez propounds, with its emphasis on "the preferential option for the poor," or the doing of justice as the only validation of belief in God, and so on. Gutiérrez's biblical writings (especially *A Theology of Liberation, On Job: The Suffering of the Innocent and God-Talk*, and his recent *The God of Life*) make clear that his great power is grounded in his biblical perspective. Would that Protestants understood a tradition-centered Catholic theology as well as Gutiérrez understands a biblically-centered Protestant theology.

While Gutiérrez has had his problems with Rome, they have not issued in formal condemnations or silencings. Not so fortunate has been Leonardo Boff, a Brazilian Franciscan, who has twice been "silenced" by Rome, meaning not allowed to speak, write, or publish for defined periods of time. In Boff's case, the issue is not so much Marxism as his presumed challenge to church authority. Boff writes extensively about the Holy Spirit, a theme that can only make defenders of hierarchy nervous, for the Holy Spirit in Christian theology is a way of understanding God that claims that we can *never* fully "understand" God, or (to put it another way) confine God within our finite and warped ways of thinking. So when Boff writes enthusiastically about the base communities as actions of the Holy Spirit, he is issuing an implicit (and sometimes explicit) criticism of the hierarchy for its unwillingness to affirm these patent outpourings of the Spirit's guidance and protection. There is a deep-seated fear that the base communities will become a rival church, and leave the One Holy Catholic and Apostolic Church to join a pretender to the claim. We have already contested the accuracy of this charge, and the fact that it is periodically leveled at Boff may say more about what is going on within fearful curia-based hearts than what is actually going on in stout community-based hearts. (Since the above was written, Boff has resigned from the priesthood and the Franciscan order but remains an active lay person within the church.)

There is another source of conflict. It is not a conflict within the church but a conflict between the church (especially liberation theologians and base community members) and the state. Those who try to apply themes of liberation theology to their surrounding locales frequently end up dead. The Introduction to this book, "Situating Ourselves," gives ample testimony to the cost that is frequently paid for moving from reflection to action. Here we see most clearly that the common thread of the above critiques is that they are fearful of change because it will create conflict—change of the inner heart, change of the intellect, change of the structures, and even change of "received" ways of stating the faith.

In order to be descriptively fair, we must also recognize the role of right-wing Protestant fundamentalist sects. (This is not a critique of mainline Protestant groups or individual Protestants who have been active in ecumenical liberation concerns, such as José Miguez-Bonino, Elsa Tamez, Emilio Castro, and Gustavo Parajón). Various TV evangelists from the United States have made Central America a primary target of their evangelizing, and backed by lavish resources, they have been promoting a gospel that specifically discourages engagement in political or economic issues and concentrates on the promises of an other-worldly heaven. There is sometimes an emphasis on *individual* morality (no drinking, for example) that can be creatively transforming. But no connections are made between faith and the need to challenge corrupt social structures. Such escapist theologies render their adherents immune from political persecution, since those with power are immensely pleased that their public policies escape serious scrutiny from the ecclesiastical right wing. This is at least one reason why the sectarians are growing faster than other church groups in Central

America. There is some evidence that where base communities are strong, the fundamentalist sects have less appeal.

Themes of conflict are disturbing and often dispiriting themes, calculated to sap our energy and cloud our vision. At such times, it is particularly important to keep hearing from those who have been involved in conflict and have managed to emerge with their clarity and commitment intact.[10] Archbishop Romero is particularly noteworthy in this respect, and it is not hard to discover the inner core of his courage or what he did with it. We have begun each chapter with a quotation from him, taken from *The Violence of Love*. This time we will end with one as well:

> When we leave Mass,
> we ought to go out
> the way Moses descended Mount Sinai:
>> with his face shining,
>> with his heart brave and strong,
>>> to face the world's difficulties.

5

Can There Be a New Way
for Us? (1)

(liberation theology and North America)

> We know that every effort to better society, especially
> when injustice and sin are so ingrained, is an effort that
> God blesses, that God wants, that God demands of us.
> —Archbishop Romero

> If we want the violence to stop, we have to go to the
> root of the disease. And here is the root: social
> injustice.
> —Archbishop Romero, again

Where does all this leave us?

Pretty far removed, it would seem, at first or even
second glance. Liberation theology is about "the God of
the poor"—and we are not poor. It's about "the view from
below"—and we're on top. It's about "good news to the
poor"—and that's bad news to the rich. It's about the
third world—and we live in the first world. It's about
social structures as carriers of evil—and those same social
structures are very beneficial to us. It's about "subversion"—and that's simply an unacceptable word in our
circles.

We can pinpoint this confusion and defensiveness by
studying the picture on the cover of this volume.[1]

If the picture showed *shepherds* at the Bethlehem stable,
most Latin Americans would be able to identify with it, for
they would know that shepherds are symbols of the poor.

Poor people, looking at such a picture, could reflect, "We are welcome there!"

Many North Americans, however, would have initial difficulty. "We are *not* poor," they might reflect, "so perhaps we are not welcome."

Let us reverse the roles. If the picture showed *kings* at the Bethlehem stable (as the picture on the cover of this book does), many North Americans might be able to identify with it, for they know that kings are symbols of power and wealth. So rich people, looking at such a picture could reflect, "We are welcome there!"

Most Latin Americans, however, would have initial (and ongoing) difficulty. "We are *not* rich," they might reflect, "so perhaps we are not welcome."

But before long, the North Americans would begin to have second thoughts: What is *really* going on at the manger scene? Are the kings being commended for their wealth? Are they agreeing to be Honorary Chairpersons of a Committee to Distribute Christmas Baskets to the Poor? Are they being told, "You have worked hard; you deserve every cent you have made"?

In each case the answer would be "No!" The rich and powerful are *not* being congratulated for their wealth; they are voluntarily surrendering a portion of their wealth. Instead of poor people bowing to them, they are bowing to poor people; Mary and Joseph and the baby were certainly not part of the Nazareth Five Hundred. Instead of poor people going to a palace to learn a few facts of life about wealth and power, rich people are coming to a stable to *un*learn a few things about wealth and power.

Let us not sentimentalize, however. Can we imagine any contemporary world leader voluntarily surrendering a significant amount of his or her power, or promising to use it only for creative ends? More to the point, can we imagine *ourselves* voluntarily surrendering the very little power we possess?

The painting's value for us lies in its insistence on a radical shift in perspective, a shift we must try to maintain for the balance of this book. So far, we have been trying to see things through the eyes of the poor. With what we have learned from them, we must now try to see things through our own eyes, and test what the new perspective means for our lives in the world today.

A few years back, when railroad grade crossings were the norm, a warning sign always gave motorists three bits of advice: Stop, Look, and Listen. Such warnings are appropriate as we begin to relate liberation theology to our situation.

Stop . . .

The initial advice is the easiest to give and the hardest to follow. We *do* need at least to slow down for a few moments in order to take stock of where we are, and we cannot do so while we are on the run. In reordering our world we are confronting potential help, but we are also confronting actual challenge. We cannot afford to neglect either.

. . . Look . . .

When Christopher Wren, the architect of Saint Paul's Cathedral in London, died, someone proposed creating a monument to his memory within the cathedral. Wiser heads prevailed, and his grave contains only the words: *Si monumentum requiris, circumspice* (If you want a monu-

ment, look about you). In our own time, when traffic
outside Saint Paul's has acquired the dimensions of un-
controllable chaos and there are only two categories of
pedestrians—the quick and the dead—it was once sug-
gested that an almost identical legend be emblazoned
above the exit doors: *Nisi monumentum requiris, circumspice*
(Unless *you* want a monument, look about you!).

The stakes are just as high when we "look about [us]"
today, particularly when we cast our gaze in the direction
of the third world. Failure to do so can, like leaving Saint
Paul's, become a matter of life and death, if not for us then
surely for numberless people in whose deaths we will be
implicated. Let their eyes become our eyes for a few
moments. What do we see?

Looking south from the United States, for example, we
see a vast area that for centuries was under the political,
economic, and ecclesiastical domination of Spain, and is
now under the more recent but rapidly growing domination of the United States. Decisions about the future of a
given country are not made in that country's capital, but
in the United States' capital, and they are made not on the
basis of what is good for the country, but on the basis of
what is good for the United States. If a country tries to
disengage from this control, there are a number of dissua-
sions that can be exerted by "the giant of the north."

Historically, one of the most frequent responses was to
"send in the Marines," who, for example, occupied Nicaragua for many years. Another tactic was to *finance and help
engineer military coups* against governments who were not
acquiescing to the wishes of the United States, as for
example, the overthrow of the democratic Arbenz government in Guatemala in 1954, and U.S. help in overthrow-

ing the democratically elected Allende government in Chile in 1970, replacing it with the ruthless dictatorship of General Pinochet, whose bloodbath reprisals took thousands of innocent Chilean lives, lives whose blood is on our hands. Ongoing *so-called "covert" military aid* has been widely made available to those who would serve U.S. interests, as, for example, our financing for ten years of the corrupt army in a civil war in El Salvador, and the arming for almost as long of the contra forces in Nicaragua, who employed widespread terrorist tactics to try to dislodge the Sandinista government. We were willing to make *assassination attempts* on rulers of countries we did not approve of, as in the case of many bungled CIA-sponsored attempts to murder Fidel Castro and make it look like an accident. We also engaged in *direct military invasion* of small countries who were not willing (in President Reagan's phrase) to "say uncle" to Uncle Sam, as, for example, in the case of Grenada and Panama, a tactic that was always being threatened against Nicaragua.

In addition to such political and military pressures, the most powerful pressure was the one most easily hidden from all but its victims—*economic pressure*. Through a variety of instrumentalities who offered "funding," many countries in Latin America ended up hopelessly in debt to the United States and other powers in the northern hemisphere, who in the 1970s made loans at interest rates impossible for poor and struggling nations to meet. It was not uncommon for the interest due each year to exceed the entire budget of a country. Economic pressures have also been exerted through restrictions on trade, high tariffs, and direct economic blockades, as in the case of Nicaragua, to such a degree that the United States virtually "bought" the 1989 election by making clear that only if the Sandinistas were defeated would the U.S. trade embargo be lifted.

In the light of such a history it is not surprising that zeal for "capitalism" is not excessive south of the Rio Grande. Whether rightly or wrongly, it is seen by many as the driving force behind all of the above—a mode of economic control that consistently benefits a few on the top at the cost of destroying the many on the bottom.

This is but a small sampling of things we need to "see" clearly. Whether or not we accept the full overlay of reasons *why* these things are so, *that* they are perceived as so is a reality we have to take seriously.

There are two other realities we have to "see," of a slightly different order:

The third world in the first world

We have been employing distinctions (first world/third world and so forth) that are easily susceptible to distortion. We need particularly to remember that the "third world" (a symbol for situations of poverty and oppression) is not just thousands of miles to the south of us or many thousands of miles to our west. It is in our midst as well, present in every U.S. city. Not too far from our museums are the substandard and decaying housing units; not too far from our schools are the drug rings and, barely in their shadow, the drug lords who consider human life cheap; not too far from our parks are the skid rows reserved for an abandoned humanity; not too far from our libraries are the sweatshops where workers (mostly women) receive far below the minimum wage; not too far from our skyscrapers (symbols of corporate power) are the soup kitchens. The third world is present in the first world.

This means that when we "listen to the third world" we must also listen to voices that are simply around the corner or down the block, for if liberation theology is a creation of the poor and oppressed, it follows that there will be many expressions of liberation theology at home as well as abroad.

As a safeguard against escapist thinking, let us remind ourselves that almost every oppressed group within our own culture has been developing its own theology of liberation. The earliest and most distinctively North American version is *black theology*, first given public recognition in James Cone's *A Black Theology of Liberation* (1970) and now forming alliances with black theologies on the continent of Africa. *Feminist* and *womanist theology*, born out of the oppression of women in the United States, has also become global; women in different parts of the world are developing both distinctive and common agendas. *Gays and lesbians* now theologize out of their particular experience of oppression and diminishment in the dominant culture. *Native American theology* is helping another victimized group gain a new sense of personhood and worth. Filipino-Americans, Hispanic-Americans, Asian-Americans, and other ethnic and racial groups, have discovered their distinctiveness, and the consequent need to find new ways to articulate the gospel from a variety of backgrounds and perspectives.

The issue of power

One large group in our society is still unaccounted for: white males, who share the dubious distinction that the groups just named look upon them as quintessential "oppressors." As a class, white males can claim to be "oppressed" themselves only by redefining the meaning of words.

Trying to guard against defensiveness (I am, after all, a birthright member of this group), I offer two comments. First, white males must accept the truth of the charges that we have been overbearing, destructive, insensitive, sexist, and racist. To the degree that such acknowledgments usher us into a newly sensitized state, we must begin to find ways to redress the wrongs we have committed. This will be a lifelong undertaking, because one does not shed the role of "oppressor" in a fortnight. Second, there is another dynamic at work as well. One reason the indictment of white males is so convincing is that, for whatever historical reasons, *white males have had the power* and have provided empirical evidence that Lord Acton was on target when he said, "Power tends to corrupt and absolute power corrupts absolutely." Is it not true that the abuse of power, at least as much as skin color or ideology, has fueled our unenviable track record? Furthermore, we have been able to mold social structures in such a way that they become our means of retaining power for ourselves, and are skewed to make it difficult for others to dislodge us. Thus race, gender, and class become intertwined with structures of power.

There is a complicating factor, however. It is that people from other racial, ethnic, and class groups are *also* susceptible to the abuse of power: a Scot (though it hurts me to say it) can be racist; a black preacher can be sexist; a woman in a position of executive responsibility can be ruthless. No one, not even a white male, has a sheer monopoly on the abuse of power; the capacity to inflict harm on others is present within us all. This makes it impossible either to confer unblemished sanctity on any racial, social, or class group or to deny the possibility of virtue to such groups.

This apparently fair-minded contention can, however, be used dishonestly as a rationale to *oppose* social change. To say "the oppressed, when they get power, always become oppressors" may have a certain amount of historical truth behind it, but it also contains the not-so-hidden agenda that those presently in control are therefore justified in fighting to keep control since the newcomers to power can be counted on to abuse it just as much as those who have unwillingly relinquished it. And since it is much more satisfying to wield power than to lack it, those on top will be tempted to curb any movements for significant social change. Changing the names and numbers of the leaders will not in their view change the essential nature of the game.

The response to this argument is to take its *possibility* seriously but refuse to accept its *inevitability*. If Santayana is right and "those who cannot remember the past are condemned to fulfil it," we at least need alongside it a more engaging scenario that reads, "those who remember the past are privileged to redirect it." The special task of the church in such situations is to *remind* all participants in the power struggle that whoever gains power will be tempted to abuse it, and also *challenge* all participants to remember that the acquisition of power can sometimes be a way to advance the common good. There is no inexorable law that decrees failure in such an endeavor, any more than there is an inexorable law that assures success. Power is not evil per se; it is necessary to any ordering of society, and it is not wrong to seek it.

Once gained, however, it is terribly hard to share, and this is what has made the role of the United States (where almost all policymakers are white males) so destructive. We, as a nation, are not willing to share power, even with very small nations (as we have cataloged only a few pages back), and this is an ultimately divisive social fact: while it may be the legitimate goal of small nations to acquire power, it is the obligation of large nations to share power. To struggle for the common good—a minority opinion in the conventional marketplace of ideas—is an extremely important act of "liberation" for power-conscious white males.

. . . and Listen

We can look and look and look (as we have been doing) and still remain adroit enough to be impervious to what is staring us in the face, particularly when we don't want to see it. For this reason, it is important to "listen" as well as to "look." It is hard to avoid hearing what is said to us, since someone else is controlling the sound waves. About the most we can do if we don't like the message is to practice the bottom line of denial—absolutely ignoring the messenger, and if that doesn't work, blaming the messenger for bad news rather than the message itself.

Such tactics must be disavowed in the present instance, for those to whom we are asked to listen can be neither ignored nor blamed. They are, most simply, our sisters and brothers in Christ, part of a worldwide fellowship to which we all belong, called the church.

What are they saying to us?

I believe they are trying to communicate to us that as things stand now, *we are part of the problem rather than part of the solution.* We are perceived (sometimes in despairing and sometimes in strident tones) as being direct contributors to the plight of the poor, and when we hear them we have to acknowledge the truth of what they are saying. Let us "listen" to three examples.

Example one

A group of American college students has gone to Recife, Brazil, for the summer, to work with the poor. The dynamic archbishop of Recife, Dom Hélder Câmara, greets them with surprising honesty, saying in effect: We are glad to have you here and hope it is a good experience. I have two requests. First, don't try to start a revolution for us, as some of your enthusiastic friends frequently wish to do. If real bullets begin to fly, your embassy will have you safely on the next plane home, and it will be our young people who get killed. Second, if you *really* want to help us, observe and learn what you can, and then go home and find ways to make your government get its boots off the necks of our people, because those boots are the main source of our misery. The problem isn't only in Recife, it's in Washington as well.

Example two

One need not travel far in Latin America to discover how widespread this conviction is, and how deep are its historical roots. Here, for example, chosen almost at random, is an appraisal of U.S. domination in Central America in 1912. A Nicaraguan bishop is writing to a U.S. cardinal, James Gibbons:

> Unfortunate mistakes have placed our country, Nicaragua, in special circumstances which deprive it of much of its autonomy, putting it under foreign influences. My

> beloved brother, your large country has made our
> small country feel the brunt of its money and its men;
> and your strong country with its battleships and its
> powerful cannons has dominated our weak country;
> and the bankers of the north have built their fortunes on
> our depleted treasuries, using extortionate loans, unjust
> treaties and unfair contracts.[2]

This could stand as a one-paragraph summary of the nature
of the basic perception of the relationship of the United
States to almost any country in Central and South America,
before and since 1912, up to the present moment.

Example three

One portion of a document, *Kairos Central America* (to
which we will shortly refer), from Christians in Central
America, lays out directly some truths about themselves
and ourselves that we need to hear:

The writers are looking for "signs of the kingdom,"
places where, even in the midst of the present human
tragedy, God is at work. The major sign for them is that
the poor become subjects of their history, rather than pawns,
objects, subhuman and expendable. The poor are now
organizing to acquire power; they are "servants of Jah-
weh" who redeem oppressive situations by their suffering and their struggle. They join Mary in proclaiming that
the mighty will be cast down from their thrones and the
poor lifted up. They announce that God is on the side of
the oppressed and will help them in their ongoing bid for
freedom. They remember that Jesus himself was born and
lived among the poor and ministered to them. They believe that they are not alone in their struggle, but are
participants in the ongoing biblical story of God's opting
for the poor.

But there are also "signs of the *anti*-kingdom," realities that are clearly opposed to God's will and must be opposed by God's children. They see the hand of our nation at work in such things as the legitimization of conquest and genocide; the equation of faith with domination and oppression; puppet governments that falsely represent themselves as something other than what they are; forms of transnational capitalism that exploit rather than help the poor; and claims that Christians should be "above politics," which means in their situation giving silent approval to tyrannical regimes.

After this catalog of sins of omission and commission, the writers describe us as accomplices in sin against the Holy Spirit whenever we "remain entrenched in our comforts, using distance and lack of clear information as excuses to remain uninvolved." To their credit, the writers recognize that they also contribute to the anti- kingdom and that the critical eye needs to be on them as well as on others. But for all Christians, a clear choice is demanded by the times: it must be "an option for the poor." Their delineation of the choices is addressed to all:

> You are on the side of the people or you become an accomplice of their oppressors; you are on the side of the poor or you are with the Empire; [you are] with the God of Life or with the idols of death.[3]

It's *Kairos* Time . . .

We will now try to relate liberation theology to our own situation by reference to a biblical word that has become a byword in the third world, the word *kairos*.[4]

We must approach it through another Greek word, *chronos*. With a little luck or ingenuity we might figure out correctly that *chronos* has something to do with time, for from it we get such time-oriented words as "chronology" and "chronometer." *Chronos* time is "clock time," the succession of seconds, minutes, hours, days, and weeks that we experience day in and day out—and sometimes through the night as well. No one is more aware of *chronos* than the insomniac.

Kairos, by contrast, points to another kind of time—a special time, a time of decision, a time when things may hang in the balance and what we do (or don't do) will have far-reaching consequences. Jesus' earliest recorded words are, "The *kairos* is fulfilled and the kingdom of God is at hand," which is not only an announcement but a call for response, since the verse continues, "repent and believe the good news" (Mark 1:15, author's translation). Paul likewise tells us to "redeem the *kairos*," to make something of a moment fraught with possibilities for good or evil.

A more homey illustration of the meaning of this important word is contained in an experience the Protestant theologian Paul Tillich had shortly after fleeing Hitler's Germany and coming to the United States. A seminarian, thinking that Professor Tillich ought to learn something about American culture, took him to a baseball game. Tillich had some trouble catching on ("Ze oompire has too much power"), and was baffled at the crowd's noisy celebration in the seventh inning, when with one out and men on first and second, the batter hit a line drive directly to the shortstop, who caught it and ran over to touch second base, completing an unassisted double play. "Vat is happening?" Tillich wanted to know. The student made several unsuccessful forays into the intricacies of double plays ("When a ball is caught before it hits the ground . . ., When a base runner fails to return to the bag after a line drive . . ."). In his extremity, he finally said, "Dr. Tillich, that was the shortstop's *kairos*." Tillich beamed. All was now clear.

A time of *kairos* is a time when unexpected possibilities enter the scene, brand new things can happen—and frequently do. Central Americans, for example, discover themselves living in a situation with almost unprecedented possibilities for change that they describe as follows (italics mine):

> Never before in our history have *the poor* felt themselves so moved by the Wind of the Spirit to be effective instruments for the purposes of the God who is Creator of all. Never before have *the churches* of Central America felt themselves so engaged and challenged by the God of the poor. Never before has *the Empire* [i.e., the first world and especially the United States] had to turn so irrationally to "might makes right." Never before has *the world* had such a generalized feeling of international solidarity and shared responsibility in the face of what is in play in Central America, in the face of what this land is giving birth to for the sake of a New Humanity and a new world.
>
> This is the moment. The hour is decisive.

An either/or situation has developed, as the writers of the document go on to recognize:

> Central America has become a *Kairos* of unforeseeable consequences: either we close the door on the possibility of hope for the poor for many years, or as prophets we open up a new Day for humanity and thus for the church. (italics mine)[5]

In formal as well as exuberant ways, the *kairos* theme has become normative in many different situations. In 1985, a large group of South Africans, from all races and denominations, issued a brave and prophetic manifesto, called *The Kairos Document*, that was one catalyst for the amazing changes that have been taking place in their country. Two years later a similar document, *Kairos Central America* (from which the above quotations are taken) was issued, dealing particularly with the struggles of small Latin American nations and their manipulation by the United States, and in 1989 *The Road to Damascus: Kairos and Conversion*, appeared with signatories from Africa, Asia, and Central America, pointing out, among other things, that struggles over allegiance to false gods characterized life within the churches as well as struggles between the church and the world. (Preliminary drafts of *kairos* documents from Europe and the United States have also been issued, too late for sustained treatment in the present volume.) An excerpt from *The Road to Damascus* captures the perspective that characterizes them all:

> God is on the side of the poor, the oppressed, the persecuted. When this faith is proclaimed and lived in a situation of political conflict between the rich and the poor, and when the rich and the powerful reject this faith and condemn it as heresy, we can read the signs and discern something more than a crisis. We are faced with a *kairos*, a moment of truth, a time for decision, a time of grace, a God-given opportunity for conversion and hope.[6]

It hardly needs pointing out that these are not themes at the forefront of the agenda of North American middle-class churches. And our friends from elsewhere are telling us that if we ignore such concerns, we will miss the *kairos* and fail to rise to its challenge.

Perhaps the most impressive fact about the *kairos* documents is the way they combine stern denunciation of the present order of things (based on careful social analysis as well as justifiable passion) and a glowing, hopeful view of the future (based on reading the present situation with eyes of faith).

The idols of this world are exposed in all of their demonic power—the worship of money, power, national-ism, privilege, and pleasure; the frenetic grasping for security; the ease of resorting to scapegoating; the fanati-cism; the lies—an analysis so realistic that it would tempt all but the most hardy to throw in the towel.

But in the midst of the "denunciation" comes what Paulo Freire has contrasted as "annunciation": the further resources that God provides, the ever-present possibility of *our* conversion from worship of the false gods to wor-ship of the true God. The Central American document concludes with the words:

> Dear sisters and brothers, we sign this *Kairos Central America* document in the name of Christ and of our people. We reaffirm, together with you, our intentions of praying, working and struggling toward carrying out of the proposals made herein, so that peace can come to our Central American peoples and to the world. We pray that the grace of God's Spirit accompany our struggle for the Kingdom.[7]

And similarly, in *The Road to Damascus:*

> Because of our faith in Jesus, we are bold enough to hope for something that fulfills and transcends all hu-man expectations, namely, the Reign of God. We are even called to live with the hope that those who collab-orate with the idols of death and those who persecute us today will be converted to the God of life.[8]

It is, indeed, a time of *kairos.*

And we are going to have to fashion a response.

6

Can There Be a New Way for Us? (2)

(our own liberation theology)

> Blood soaked fields will never be fertile and bloody reforms will never bear fruit.
>
> —Archbishop Romero

> . . . every day do something
> that won't compute. Love the Lord.
> Love the world. Work for nothing.
> Take all that you have and be poor.
> Love someone who does not deserve it.
> Denounce the government and embrace
> the flag. Hope to live in that free republic for which it
>   stands.
> . . . . . .
> . . . Be joyful
> though you have considered all the facts.
> . . . .
> As soon as the generals and the politicos
> can predict the motions of your mind
> lose it. Leave it as a sign
> to mark the false trail, the way
> you didn't go. Be like the fox
> who makes more tracks than necessary,
> some in the wrong direction.
> Practice resurrection.
>
> —Wendell Berry, "Manifesto: The
>   Mad Farmer Liberation Front"[1]

This chapter has gone through many drafts. A couple of them were too harsh, and at least one was too bland. I am

sure that the draft that has survived and appears here has
its own built-in shortcomings, although I feel no obligation
to point them out. But at least it has been hard work—
which the remnants of my Calvinist upbringing suggest
may confer a little merit on it after all. We shall see.

The problem the chapter has to face is that every reader
is at a different "place," not only geographically, but
ideologically, theologically, and temperamentally. An
idea that clicks for one will be a dud for someone else.
Recognizing this, what follows is not a universally appli-
cable plan of action, but a purposefully unstructured collection of comments.

Is It *Kairos* Time for Us?

One thing that characterizes the writers of all the *kairos*
documents is their searingly honest self-scrutiny. While
they find plenty of evil in the world for which they do not
feel constrained to accept responsibility, they are at the
same time aware that some of it, at least, can be laid at
their own doorstep and that they must deal with it. A
similar awareness on our own part is surely a necessary
prelude to discerning possibilities of *kairos* for ourselves.

These lines are being written shortly after the verdict of
"not guilty" in the trial of four white policemen charged
with beating Rodney King, an African American, and the
outburst of rioting and violence in Los Angeles that followed it. I indicate this context deliberately, for I wonder
how many readers—a year later—will think, "Let's see
now, who was Rodney King?" or wonder what the "Los
Angeles riots" were all about. My own reaction is that the
two events are a defining moment in our history as a
nation—a time when the veneer around the American

way of life was stripped away and white middle-class people discovered something that African American and other minority peoples have known all along: that we are a racist society and also a violent society. At the same time that we have been denying these truths about ourselves, we have consistently denied equal educational opportunities to minorities and have thus shut them off from the possibility of meaningful employment. They become trapped in cycles of poverty from which they cannot escape, and each generation can only cast its frustrations and anger on the next. If there ever was a *"kairos* time" this is it. We are in the midst of what Kierkegaard called "the midnight hour when all must unmask," and when that happens we may not even recognize who we are.

These words are also being written in the midst of a presidential campaign that has hit an all-time low in mudslinging, innuendo, negative campaigning, cheap shots, and misleading "sound bites." This is partly due to a lack of vision, wisdom, and leadership from the White House for well over a decade, but there is a vacuum in *both* political parties when it comes to a sense of national purpose. Increasing numbers of Americans confess to experiencing a loss of faith in the ability of our democratic process to provide the kind of leadership the times demand. It is a safe guess that this disenchantment will not decrease but intensify.

This sense of national *malaise* resonates with an ongoing emphasis in the *kairos* documents on the dangers of idolatry. Our problem today is not that we as a people do not believe in God, but that we as a people have many gods from whom to choose; this lack of a true "center" is one reason for our plight. Idolatry, or the worship of false gods, is perhaps the sin to which the Bible most often calls attention, particularly within the Hebrew scriptures. If we do try to name the chief idol in our national pantheon, it is undoubtedly some form of "nationalism." What has at times been a healthy pride in our heritage and its contributions to the entire human venture has degenerated into a crabbed insistence not only that because of our heritage we behave better than any other nation but that we also have a right to determine how other nations shall behave.

The more we fear that the *malaise* is serious, the more we stoop to braggadocio in an attempt to hide the fear, forgetting G. K. Chesterton's comment that the most serious illness of all is to imagine that one is quite well. So, going Theodore Roosevelt one better, we both speak loudly *and* carry a big stick. If other nations refuse to accept *our* agenda for *their* future, we bash them—verbally (as in the case of Japan) or militarily (as in the recent cases of Grenada, Panama, and Iraq). The often unspoken but deeply held assumption to which we feel we must cling is that we are always right; *any* nation can be bashed save us. In order to assume unchallenged preeminence in the bashing department, we create inordinately expensive (and increasingly superfluous) weapon systems, at the cost of the decay of our schools, our social services, our infrastructure, and, increasingly, our environment. It is a policy under which everyone loses.

As long as the god of nationalism continues to rule us we can only anticipate more of the same: false (even unstated) goals, neglect of the needy, disregard for the truth, and lack of direction for the present, let alone the future. Only through the dethronement of the false god, and our liberation from its control over our lives, can we begin to turn the tide. Perhaps the greatest gift third world Christians could give us would be to share their concept of deity, as we have discovered it in previous pages—rather than a god of national self-aggrandizement, a God of love and justice. The distance between the two gods is the distance between replicating a past that delivered "liberty and justice for *some*," and creating a future that provides "liberty and justice for *all*."

This also suggests a way of our acting more creatively in relation to the entire human family. An area of increasing concern is our human responsibility for the environment, particularly in the larger and more "developed" countries, and our failure to take that responsibility seriously. We engage in massive dumping of toxic substances, thinning the "ozone layer" to a frightening degree, exhausting nonrenewable resources, presiding over the extinction of various types of animal life, accumulating increasing amounts of radioactive nuclear waste we simply don't know how to dispose of, and so on, leaving us with an environment less and less able to sustain human life. (One person puts it: in the third world don't drink the water; in the first world don't breathe the air.) Sober estimates of our human future predict that if we do nothing to stem this tide of exploitation and destruction, the planet will be uninhabitable in forty to one hundred years. Here, in other words, is an "issue" on which pioneer work is only beginning to be done, while the clock is running out on us. It should be possible to enlist the support of many people from different economic, racial, geographical, and class backgrounds to work on such issues, all the while remembering that countries like the United States bear the biggest responsibility for the problem and (as Mr. Bush's coercive acts at the 1992 Rio de Janeiro environmental conference attest) have so far done the least to alleviate it.

Even on this brief accounting, it is clear that we are indeed in a time of *kairos*, although one we could easily miss. Portents of disaster fill the air, signs of hope are hard to come by, and fresh agendas for the future are far from clear. Consequently one of the most important tasks for the churches is to try to "discern the signs of the times" with new urgency and depth, so that the possibilities for transformation—for "conversion," as *The Road to Damascus* document unambiguously puts it—will be more apparent. Christians are never entitled to say that any situation is totally devoid of hope, but we are also warned to heed the dangers and perplexities that lie ahead.

Three Cautions

As we try to respond, there are three comments about perspective that we must clarify.

Embracing the flag

The phrase "embrace the flag," in Wendell Berry's poem at the beginning of this chapter, may have surprised some readers. George Bush brought the phrase "embrace the flag" to high political prominence during the 1988 presidential campaign. For him it meant uncritical and unambiguous adulation of all things American. Wendell Berry's use of the phrase, in "Manifesto: The Mad Farmer Liberation Front," means something quite different, however, and he protects the phrase from profanation both fore and aft. Preceding the phrase in question, he first writes "Denounce the government," warning us to be ongoingly critical of the policies of our country. "The flag" here symbolizes what *ought to be*, in contrast to "the government," which signifies what *is*. The two must never be compressed into one, which is the primary demand of the god of nationalism. The theme is similarly illuminated in the words immediately following "embrace the flag," which read, "Hope to live in that free / republic for which it stands." Berry here suggests that the "free republic" is not yet a present achievement, and thus never to be equated with existing structures, but only a future possibility— perhaps occasionally, but only occasionally, realized in fragmentary form in the present. In both cases, the tension between what is and what ought to be is maintained—a crucial safeguard against an idolatry that is exhibited whenever the sole injunction is to "embrace the flag."

Such a perception is absolutely essential if we are to discern a *kairos* for ourselves.

Anger, not hatred

If we are to be responsive to *kairos* themes in our own situation, we will also need to cultivate a wide gap between anger and hatred in our responses.[2] We will discover much—in our own domestic life, in our country's international relations, in the ugliness of dictatorships, in the frightful ubiquity of torture—that should fill us with anger, revulsion, righteous indignation, and outrage. We *should* be angered by the specter of hungry children, by the destructiveness of war, by the way the economic system sucks the lifeblood out of the poor, by the reality of nations (our own included) using "food as a weapon." There is something the matter with us if we are not angered. We need to be able to claim anger as a virtue, for if we can remain psychically undisturbed by evil, we are letting indifference go bail for responsibility.

Hatred, however, is a very different thing. Anger can galvanize us into action for justice, whereas an act of hatred dehumanizes whoever is its recipient, making a person into an object. And to dehumanize another is to dehumanize oneself in the process. The exercise is never even a win-lose situation, but always lose-lose.

The distinction is important, for it is fatally easy for anger, which can often be creative, to slip imperceptibly into hatred, which will always be destructive.

Distinguishing the oppressor and the oppressed

We have been employing a distinction throughout this book between oppressor and oppressed. The discussion leads to a claim that the initiative in bringing about liberation lies with the oppressed, and that those most likely to deter such initiations are the oppressors. When we push further to explore just who the oppressors are, it is disturbingly clear that they are likely to be the sort of people who read this sort of book—reasonably well off, at least modestly comfortable, and on the whole satisfied with the way things are. No oppressed person is instinctively going to look on us as allies or approach us for help.

Is this the end of the discussion? I think not. At least I hope not, for we need to explore the possibility that some people can locate themselves on both sides of the hyphen that separates oppressor-oppressed.

Karen Lebacqz, a white North American feminist theologian, is particularly helpful as she describes her own ambivalent situation.[3] Precisely as "a white North American feminist theologian," she is part of the oppressor class in relation to brown or black third-world women. She has many advantages denied to them, and has access to comforts that her culture makes available to her at the cost of exploiting women elsewhere. In this sense, she can be perceived as one of the *oppressors*.

But it is also true that in her own culture (which is male-dominated in terms of public, economic, and political life, let alone church life) she is herself denied many opportunities and privileges that the society reserves for men alone, so that in this sense she is one of the *oppressed*. In her case, the ambiguity is employed creatively, giving her sensitivities she would otherwise lack, and she is able, as she says, "to temper my oppressor mentality by remembering my own experiences of oppression and by attending to the voices of the oppressed."

The case may not be so clear-cut for white North American males, but those who are sensitive discover that they, too, in addition to being "oppressors," are frequently oppressed by the socioeconomic situation in which they find themselves, with pressures abounding to make them conform to such things as striving for upward mobility, competing ruthlessly for jobs, responding to siren calls to "comfort" as the expected fruit of daily labor, checking their consciences at the entrance to the workplace, and so on—in short, worshiping the idols exposed in the *kairos* documents we have already examined. The cost of renouncing such loyalties can be great, especially the likelihood (so movingly described by Jürgen Moltmann) of being labeled "a traitor to one's class." And since "class" is one of society's most sought after icons, the willingness to court such renunciation is a crucial threshold experience.

There are no formulas for resolving these issues. But that those just described need "liberation" from the idols thrust on them by their culture is surely clear. And the sincerity (or lack thereof) of those who seek liberation for themselves and others will become evident in the way they translate words into deeds.

Some Next Steps

In the light of the realities we have sketched, the task is to create a liberation theology appropriate to where we are that will do three things: (1) help us confront our own situation and seek to understand it, (2) help us put our theological heritage and our situation into communication with one another, and (3) help us to move to actions that are appropriate to our attempts to relate the first two. How are we to go about this?

Jack Nelson-Pallmeyer, who has worked extensively in both Central and North America, has made three proposals that are simultaneously ways to get started and goals to meet. This means that they are unlikely to go out-of-date during our lifetimes. They provide a springboard for further reflection.[4]

We must consciously form communities of committed Christians

The most important thing to remember is that none of this can be done solo. We must analyze together, theologize together, strategize together, worship together, and act together. A central theme of the New Testament is that we are not to be isolated individuals but part of a community. To be "in Christ" means "to be in the Christian community." A solitary Christian is a contradiction in terms.

What we do in community must have at least three ingredients. We must engage in our own *social analysis*, learning where the real sources of power are, the actual means available for change, the ways in which our immediate society responds to challenge, and so forth—all in clear and hard-headed fashion. With new perspectives thus formed, we must also engage in *Bible study*, drawing both nourishment and further insight as we let the biblical stories become mirrors in which we see our own contemporary story in a new way. And we must also engage in *action*, translating our analysis and our biblical exposure into ways of coping with, and challenging, the world in which we are immersed.

> These components function together, forming a continuous interactive circle that should not be broken. The purpose of bible study is to encourage discipleship, not simply to know more about Jesus; the goal of social analysis is transforming action, not simply to know more about difficult social problems. Social actions are then evaluated and reformulated in the context of further bible study and social analysis.

It will be apparent even from these brief remarks that we are drawing on the experience of the base communities. The analogy is helpful provided we do not claim too much for it. For the Latin American base communities almost invariably arise out of situations of poverty and dire need, whereas our communities inevitably reflect our own more stable and secure situations. Rule Number One: Let there be no false romanticism about who we are.

Just as the Latin American base communities are still part of the overarching structure we call "church," communities that are formed here need likewise to keep the church connection for at least two reasons: first, the churches themselves need the leavening that comes from such groups; second, with whatever are our collective ecclesiastical faults, the churches are one of the few places left in our society from which impulses for liberation and change might be effectively harnessed and strengthened.

Such communities are also places where what is called "a spirituality of liberation" can be nurtured, through

Bible study, liturgy, and shared common actions, where individuals joined together begin to find empowerment that is more conventionally described as the presence of the Holy Spirit.

As people of faith, we must be willing to speak the truth to one another and to the dominant community

It is a given that we live in the midst of lies—lies about "welfare cheats," lies about our nation's true intentions in the Middle East, lies about the omnicompetence of capitalism, or any other economic system, lies about our national goals, lies about the reasons for poverty.

We must first speak the truth "to one another" so that we have our facts straight, learn from one another the most effective ways to speak the truth, and are buttressed by the fact of shared convictions, assuring us that we are not off the wall in our individual appraisals.

But we must also speak the truth "to the dominant community." Insights are wasted if shared only with the like-minded. Here particularly we need the ongoing assurance that we are not alone, that there are those who will support and substantiate our voiced concerns, and help us formulate proposals for change. The one thing of which we can be sure is that "the dominant community" will not take kindly to proposals that challenge its power, its authority structures, or its deep investment in maintaining the status quo. Those to whom the truth is addressed never want to hear the truth. Speaking the truth to the dominant community will at least not be dull.

We must take risks

Risk-taking goes with the territory of being an authentic Christian in the 1990s. (It has also gone with the territory of being an authentic Christian since about A.D. 30.) A complacent Christian is as much a contradiction in terms as a solitary Christian.

If there is anything we have learned from those with liberation concerns in the third world it is that the risks are high. There is a long list of martyrs available for any who doubt it. Most of us do not face the likelihood of being imprisoned or tortured or shot for our faith, and in our society it would be false heroics to assume so. As Alan Paton, speaking out of the South African situation said, Christians do not seek suffering. That is sick. But Christians must realize that their actions might lead to suffering as one of the costs of being faithful.

I believe there is an eleventh commandment for Christians: Thou shalt not decide that someone else should become a martyr. In the nature of the case there is no checklist of risks that can be duplicated wholesale against which Christians can measure themselves. That being said, Christians must seek to discern the kind of witness that is demanded of them, and then go with it.

On an individual level, it may be a vastly simplified life-style, or a sharing of tools among neighbors, or limiting consumption, or engaging in tax resistance as a protest against expenditures for the military, or refusing to accept induction into the armed forces, or committing oneself to nonviolence as a consistent way of life, or continuing to challenge the power structures, or refusing to build a big new church and instead making the money available for low-cost housing.

On a communal level (at least as important as the individual level), churches will increasingly have to decide whether they serve God or mammon. Will it be an uncritical "our country, right or wrong," or will it be

"Here we stand, we can do no other"? Will it be "American citizenship is our deepest loyalty as a community," or will it be "We must obey God rather than men" (Acts 5:29, one place where sexist language is still appropriate)? Will we turn our heads when politicians refuse to declare a "peace dividend," or will we join together—Catholics, Protestants, Jews, or whatever, to *demand* that an agenda for social justice be recreated? Will we collectively allow wage discrimination to flourish, or will we flex our collective muscles in defense of "equal pay for equal work"?

Both lists can be as long as the human imagination.

A Concluding Biblical Image: Servants in Pharaoh's Court

Many Latin Americans define themselves in relation to biblical images. One of the most widely utilized is the story of the liberation of the children of Israel from the tyranny of the Egyptian pharaoh, the so-called exodus from Egypt. Oppressed people today identify easily with the oppressed peoples of yesterday, the Hebrew slaves in the story. Contemporary women discover new possibilities for engaging in social transformation when they read how the Hebrew midwives outwitted the pharaoh and weakened his power over them.

Where can the rest of us make contact with this story as we seek to work for social change?

I have come to the uncomfortable conclusion that most of us who read (and write) books like this can be identified as *servants in pharaoh's court;* lower echelon folk who are nevertheless members of the establishment, with advancement possibilities if we play our cards right. This is true whether our pharaoh is the current resident in the

White House, the CEO of the corporation that employs us, the chairperson of the university department in which we are trying to get tenure, or the head of the real estate agency where we are still working only on commission. How do we relate to the society around us? How do we change it (if we wish to change it)? How, in other words, do we function as human beings? A number of options are open to us:

Option one

The easiest thing is to *accept the perks and the comforts with gratitude.* After all, by dint of hard work, family connections, or just plain luck, we've gotten where we are and we intend to stay there. The hours are good, and the pension (while less than we'd like) will be adequate. We have reasonable job security provided we get to work on time, exude efficiency, and carry out the boss's orders. If the pharaoh says "Jump!" we'll ask "How high?" and if, in another situation, he says something like "Crack down on the Jews," we'll ask, "How hard?"

The price we pay is selling our souls to the highest bidder. We let someone else manipulate the strings of our puppetlike existence.

Option two

So some of us, while realizing that our power is limited, nevertheless determine that we will try to use our position *to help others a little bit, now and then, so long as it doesn't get us in trouble.* We realize that most folks don't have the advantages we have had, and that we ought to exhibit *some* concern for their well-being as well as ours. When we discover how many people fall below the poverty line, we help by giving to a tax-exempt charitable organization.

When we discover people living near us who have no jobs, no shelter, and no food, we donate volunteer time to help set up shelters and job agencies and soup kitchens in some other part of town, so their plight won't be so desperate. When times are lean and the workers in our corporation are told, in effect, to make bricks without straw, we won't make a public protest, but we may try, behind the scenes, to persuade the overseer that the policy is going to lower production rather than increase it, and that as a result, it isn't going to make friends for either of us in the front office. Sometimes the pharaohs we serve applaud our humane gestures, and at the annual banquet we may be cited on the Honor Roll of Responsible Citizens, which gives us a nice, warm feeling.

The price we pay for adopting this position is that we are fooling ourselves; we aren't really changing *anything*. We are tinkering around the edges of a fundamentally unjust situation, making no more than cosmetic adjustments. No matter how kind we are at the soup kitchen, people are going to be hungry again in a few hours, and the soup kitchen (while, of course, necessary for *today*) won't ever solve the long-range problems of unemployment or unfair wage scales, which are what make the soup kitchens necessary.

Option three

Occasionally people become so aware of the ineffectiveness of tiny efforts like the above, and so outraged at the inequities that are part of the fabric of our society, that they decide that the fabric must be ripped off, the faulty structure under it displayed for what it really is, so that the whole system can be discarded, and we can devote ourselves to the task of rebuilding out of the debris. The metaphor should not deceive us—we are talking about *radical social change or revolution.*

Radical social change is not likely to emanate from places like Chautauqua or Beverly Hills or Webster Groves, where, on the whole, the inhabitants benefit from the inequities. (Some recent surveys claim that 1 percent of our population owns 90 percent of the wealth.) But in places like Watts or Harlem or south Chicago, where human patience has worn out, "liberal" alternatives haven't worked, and the standard of living is primitive compared to other sectors of the society, the option of revolution increasingly looks like the realistic alternative to throwing in the towel.

What readers of this book need to remember is that we, who have no burning zeal for "starting a revolution," have, as a nation, contributed mightily to the adverse conditions that make revolution attractive to others at home and abroad. Our national track record of ignoring places where poverty and injustice abound is distressingly consistent. We support dictators who will see that revolution does not erupt, whether they are named Franco or Marcos or Somoza or Pinochet or Noriega or Saddam Hussein (we lavishly supported the last two until they were no longer "useful" to us).

Only when the thin veneer of acceptance of the unacceptable wears off (as it did for many in the United States in 1992, as we mentioned a few pages back, after the announcement of the acquittal of the white Los Angeles policemen who beat African American Rodney King) do we discover how unjust are the ways we order our society by paying lip service, but no more, to such cornerstones of society as justice and compassion.

We need also to remember that there are revolutions

and revolutions. Having hung in with our third-world sisters and brothers this long, we should not only be aware that they have every right to opt for revolution to transform their own unjust situations, but that they have every right to enlist our help, not only in supporting their goals, but in changing those aspects of our own society that continue to thwart the achievement of their legitimate goals. Sometimes this will need to be done by direct confrontation, and sometimes wisdom will suggest that it be done by disengagement from evil structures (our fourth option, coming up soon), or by devising schemes to use those structures in ways their creators do not intend (the "servants in pharaoh's court" option we will examine in conclusion).

The price that is paid for embracing the revolutionary option is that the attempt might fail and the last state be worse than the first, from failing to "count the cost" ahead of time, or making overly romantic assessments of what was desirable in relation to what was possible. The price for *not* embracing the revolutionary option is that evil, unchallenged, may be able to dig its way even more firmly into ongoing and unjust power structures. To back the oppressors rather than the oppressed must be one of the worst things a Christian can do.

Option four

To someone who has been an uneasy servant in pharaoh's court, the most creative option may sometimes be *to leave the court and devote oneself to creating a better model of how human life could be lived*. In Christian history this has been called the "sectarian" position. Small bands of people get together and decide to withdraw as much as possible from the evil compromises that life in pharaoh's court demands, establishing communities where the demonic powers of government and big business and militarism can no longer overwhelm the demands of conscience. There are groups who have done this creatively, especially among the Quakers and Mennonites. They model their communities on a belief that "there is that of God within every person," that "it can never be right to destroy another human life," that "war is always wrong," and on similar commitments dismissed as "impractical" in pharaoh's court.

Yay!

The value of the witness is that it is so consistent and clear-cut that it simply cannot be ignored, especially since those who adopt it are usually willing to endure ridicule and sometimes attack, rather than yield to conventional standards of vice and virtue. Those who continue to live in pharaoh's court, where "compromise" is always the order of the day, need reminding that there *can* be what Paul called "a more excellent way," the way of love, and that certain segments of society refuse to write it off as impractical and irrelevant. It is not so much that love has failed, but that it has scarcely ever been tried.

The price that is paid for this position is that disengagement from pharaoh's court removes one from the possibility of immediate effective action within the court and allows the power of others to go unchallenged. Any impact will be long-run rather than short-term. Those who adopt this position, however, believe that the way to create a better society is to begin building it right now rather than waiting for a "propitious" time that may never come.

Option five

A final option is *to stay within pharaoh's court, conscious of all the compromises that entails, and try to be the loyal opposi-*

tion. Such persons say, "We'll work with the tools at our disposal, which are far from ideal but which are all we have, and try to bend social structures toward more justice rather than less, and when Pharaoh makes moral decisions that do not deserve support, we will try to speak a clear no rather than a reluctant yes."

Before and during the recent Gulf War, for example, almost all the mainline Catholic and Protestant church leaders opposed both the arms buildup that preceded the war and the consequent military action. Their task from within pharaoh's court was to try to "speak truth to power." In that particular case, of course, power (in the person of George Bush) took no heed. That is not necessarily a reason to give up being "the loyal opposition," but simply a stark indication of the need to try harder and learn from the defeat. For in the aftermath of the war, the church leaders appear closer to the truth than the White House leaders: the war's objectives (never clearly stated) were not achieved, the American public was continuously and consciously deceived both by the White House and the Pentagon, and the massive human suffering occasioned by the war was an immoral price to pay for so-called victory. The voice of the church was needed then and will clearly be needed in the future, as similar morally bankrupt actions are proposed by pharaoh's court, which seems never to learn from past mistakes.

Those who work within pharaoh's court, however, must always remember that a time may come, and probably will, when the demands of Christian witness may dictate a total break with pharaoh in order to witness even more vigorously "on the outside." Deciding just when that moment has come is difficult, and individuals can legitimately make it at different times.

The price for being "the loyal opposition" is the danger of selling out too soon to what is expedient or what the public will tolerate, and ending up as accomplices of evil.

"Loyal opposition" initially means being loyal to pharaoh through opposition to some, but by no means all, of his policies. But in any showdown, being loyal to God will mean increasing opposition to pharaoh.

If that's not clear, just ask Moses.

Study Questions

Introduction: Situating Ourselves

1. Put yourself in the situation of any of the persons described in the Introduction. What would this do to your faith in God? To your faith in your fellow human beings? To your sense that the situation could be significantly changed?

2. What is your overall estimate of the role of the United States in the lives of these Latin Americans?

3. How do you account for the reality of joy and hope in the lives of these people? What inklings do you get of how their faith could persuade them that liberation is a possibility?

Chapter One: A New Way of Understanding People

1. How can we enter into the lives and experiences of those whose circumstances are so different from our own?

2. What difference does it make whether we think primarily of "persons" or "concepts" in working for social change?

3. What are the characteristics of *compromiso* (commitment) and hope?

4. How can we relate belief in "God in the midst" to a "preferential option for the poor"?

Chapter Two: A New Way of Seeing the World

1. Which of the two versions of the "Columbus story" speaks more to you? Which version seems to you to do more justice to the facts?

2. In examining the main results of the "discovery" of the new world, how do you balance the "good" consequences against the "evil" ones?

3. How do you explain the radical "conversion" of Bartolomé de las Casas? What would be a contemporary example of such an about-face? What are the most important things we learn from him?

4. Juan Luis Segundo says that unless we agree that "the world should not be the way it is," we will never understand liberation theology. Do you agree or disagree? Why is this starting point so important?

5. Does social analysis have any role to play in theology? Is "change from above" all that bad? Is "change from below" all that good? Can we relate human utopias to the kingdom of God without selling one or the other short?

Chapter Three: A New Way of Encountering God

1. Why has the United States been so fearful of social change in the Southern Hemisphere?

2. The chapter suggests six ways in which Latin Americans reflect on what it means to "encounter God." What does each of these approaches say (or fail to say) to you as you proceed on your own faith journey?

3. Can you offer an illustration out of our own culture of a "praxis situation"?

4. What does John Robertson mean for us when he says that "God has yet more light to break forth from his holy word"?

5. An important question: What are the three "levels" of the liberation message? An even more important question: How are they interrelated?

6. What is the difference between "a Christology from above" and a "Christology from below"? What difference does the difference make?

Chapter Four: A New Way of Being the Church

1. What is the significance of such milestones as "Vatican II," "Medellín," and "Puebla" on the church's pilgrimage to the modern world?

2. What things have characterized the "base communities" in their rapid ascendancy in the life of the church? What kind of carryover value do they have for us?

3. What things are most significant about the Latin American use of the Bible? To what extent are such approaches transferable to our North American situation?

4. Is a "militant reading" of scripture possible in middle-class white churches?

5. Is conflict in the church always negative? In what ways can it be a sign of new vitality?

Chapter Five: Can There Be a New Way for Us? (1)

1. What are some of the ways in which the United States has tried to impose its will on Latin America?

2. What are the realities of "the third world within the first world"? How can we be sensitive to them?

3. Is it possible to use power creatively without being betrayed by it?

4. Create arguments for and against the contention that "we are part of the problem rather than part of the solution." Where do you think the truth lies?

5. What are the true "signs of the kingdom" and "signs of the anti-kingdom"? Does such an analysis lead to hope or despair?

6. What are the most persuasive indicators that we live in a *kairos* situation? (It will help in answering this question to clarify first of all the meaning of the word *kairos*.)

Chapter Six: Can There Be a New Way for Us? (2)

1. Is it appropriate to describe our present situation as one of *malaise* (discomfort and unrest), or would the national ethos be better served by optimistic reports?

2. What are the characteristics of idols as opposed to the true God? Is the idol of nationalism a real threat to our nation's future?

3. Can white middle-class people have any inkling of what it means to be "oppressed"? What would be the creative possibilities of such an identification, however marginal?

4. Discuss each of the three "next steps" outlined in the text. What *specific* actions could characterize each of them?

5. Are there significant connections between "speaking the truth" and "risk-taking"? Provide some examples.

6. Using the image of being "servants in pharaoh's court," refine the strong and weak points of each option discussed in the text. Where do you find yourself along the spectrum? Are you open to ongoing repositioning?

Notes and Resources

Introduction: Situating Ourselves

1. The vignettes are rewritten (and condensed) versions of material initially published on the occasion of my return from various trips to Latin America, in *Christianity and Crisis, Christian Century, Commonweal,* and *Our Sunday Visitor.* The incident in the Buenos Aires airport is adapted from my *Creative Dislocation* (Nashville: Abingdon Press, 1980).

Chapter One: A New Way of Understanding People

1. Each chapter is headed by a brief quotation from Archbishop Oscar Arnulfo Romero, *The Violence of Love: The Pastoral Wisdom of Archbishop Oscar Romero* (New York: Harper & Row, 1988). Romero was a conservative Salvadoran bishop who (perhaps for that reason) was made head of the Salvadoran hierarchy in 1977. Partly because of the brutal killing of one of his priests, Fr. Rutilio Grande, S.J.— whose "crime" was helping village people form a cooperative—Romero was converted to the cause of the poor and became their advocate. He issued increasing challenges to the corrupt Salvadoran government, which was more interested in consolidating power than dispensing justice.

It was a collision course from the beginning, with an expected outcome: Romero was murdered in March 1980 while saying mass. Shortly before his death he said, "If they kill me, I shall rise again in the Salvadoran people."

He has.

A friend questioned the extensive use of Romero's comments: "All those things were said during the Salvadoran war. But the war is over now, and it's time to look ahead rather than back." I both concur and dissent. Precisely because the war *is* over, many people will argue for "business as usual," accepting the social injustices that occasioned the war and did not disappear when the war ended. In the deepest sense, "the war goes on," as the rich continue their attempts to get even richer at the expense of the poor. It is good news that the military encounters are now infrequent, but the economic battles continue unabated, and Romero's words are needed more than ever.

The fullest and most reliable biography is James Brockman's *Romero: A Life* (Maryknoll, N.Y.: Orbis Books, 1989). Romero's *Voice of the Voiceless* (Maryknoll, N.Y.: Orbis Books, 1985) contains the texts of Romero's four "pastoral letters" to the Salvadoran people, still as powerful as when they were first written.

2. Gustavo Gutiérrez is frequently referred to in this and all the succeeding chapters. My supreme debt is to him, not only for the clarity of his witness but for the commitment of his life. His *A Theology of Liberation*, rev. ed. (Maryknoll, N.Y.: Orbis Books, 1988), originally published in Spanish in 1971, is by any standard of measurement the most important single book about liberation theology. I have offered my own exposition and tribute in *Gustavo Gutiérrez: An Introduction to Liberation Theology* (Maryknoll, N.Y.: Orbis Books, 1990), from which I shall occasionally draw in the pages that follow.

Chapter Two: A New Way of Seeing the World

1. Bartolomé de las Casas is a fairly recent "discovery" on the part of North Americans who have usually been

nourished only by the Columbus story. The material about him in this chapter is condensed from my article "*1492: Another Legacy*," in *Christianity and Crisis*, January 13, 1992.

The following are the most easily accessible Las Casas resources in English: Las Casas, *The Devastation of the Indies: A Brief Account*, trans. Herma Briffault (Baltimore and London: Johns Hopkins University Press, 1992); George Sanderlin, ed., *Witness: Writings of Bartolomé de las Casas*, introduction by Gustavo Gutiérrez (Maryknoll, N.Y.: Orbis Books, 1992); Las Casas, *The Only Way*, ed. Helen Rand Parish (Mahwah, N.J.: Paulist Press, 1992). The fullest available work in English about Las Casas is Juan Freide and Benjamin Keen, eds., *Bartolomé de las Casas in History* (De Kalb: Northern Illinois University Press, 1971). An account of the issues at stake in the Las Casas/Sepúlveda debate is contained in Lewis Hanke, *Aristotle and the American Indians* (Bloomington and London: Indiana University Press, 1974).

Gutiérrez has done a great deal to bring Las Casas to the attention of the theological world. He is completing a huge historical and theological appraisal, one part of which has appeared in Spanish: Gutiérrez, *Dios o el oro en las Indias* (Lima: C.E.P., 1990). There are further materials by Gutiérrez on Las Casas in English in Gustavo Gutiérrez and Richard Shaull, *Liberation and Change* (Atlanta: John Knox Press, 1977); Sergio Torres and Virginia Fabella, eds., *The Emergent Gospel* (Maryknoll, N.Y.: Orbis Books, 1976); Gustavo Gutiérrez, *The Power of the Poor in History* (Maryknoll, N.Y.: Orbis Books, 1983).

2. Las Casas, *The Devastation of the Indies*, pp. 29, 31.

3. Paulo Freire's theme of "conscientization" is developed seminally in his *Pedagogy of the Oppressed* (New York:

Herder & Herder, 1972). The book is not easy reading, partly because it demands that we start thinking in brand new ways. I have tried to sift through some of this material in *Gustavo Gutiérrez*, pp. 65–69.

4. The material on Gutiérrez's treatment of poverty can be supplemented by reading his "Poverty: Solidarity and Protest," in *Theology of Liberation*, ch. 13.

5. The above paragraphs on poverty are adapted from my *Gustavo Gutiérrez: An Introduction to Liberation Theology*, p. 32.

Chapter Three: A New Way of Encountering God

1. The quotation from Henri Nouwen is found in his *¡Gracias!* (New York: Harper & Row, 1983), pp. 174–175.

2. The image of theology as a love letter is found in Gutiérrez, *Theology of Liberation*, p. xlvi.

3. The "three levels of liberation" need constantly to be stressed as interconnected, since critics (perversely, I believe) are always trying to suggest that liberation theology is only concerned about social structures. The theme is important enough for Gutiérrez to refer to it on three separate occasions in *Theology of Liberation* (pp. 24–25, 103–104, and 107) and more extensively in a later work, *The Truth Shall Make You Free* (Maryknoll, N.Y.: Orbis Books, 1990), pp. 121–136. My own exposition above is drawn from my *Spirituality and Liberation* (Philadelphia: Westminster Press, 1988), pp. 121–122.

4. On the overall issues of this chapter (and this book) help can be gotten from a number of interpretative works, of which the following are only a sampling:

Phillip Berryman, *Liberation Theology* (New York: Pantheon Press, 1987)

Edward Cleary, *Crisis and Change: The Church in Latin America Today* (Maryknoll, N.Y.: Orbis Books, 1985)

Alfred T. Hennelly, ed., *Liberation Theology: A Documentary History* (Maryknoll, N.Y.: Orbis Books, 1990)

Deane William Ferm, *Profiles in Liberation: Thirty-Six Portraits of Third World Theologians* (Mystic, Conn.: Twenty-Third Publications, 1988)

Arthur McGovern, *Liberation Theology and Its Critics* (Maryknoll, N.Y.: Orbis Books, 1989)

Craig L. Nessen, *Orthopraxis or Heresy: The North American Response to Liberation Theology* (Decatur, Ga.: Scholars Press, 1989)

The following books examine liberation roots in earlier Christian history:

Richard Shaull, *The Reformation and Liberation Theology* (Louisville, Ky.: Westminster/John Knox Press, 1991)

John de Gruchy, *Liberating Reformed Theology: A South African Contribution to an Ecumenical Debate* (Grand Rapids: Eerdmans, 1991)

Dorothee Soelle, *Thinking About God: An Introduction to Theology* (Philadelphia: Trinity Press International, 1990)

Daniel S. Schipani, ed., *Freedom and Discipleship: Liberation Theology in an Anabaptist Perspective* (Maryknoll, N.Y.: Orbis Books, 1989)

For information from "non-theological" sources about the political and economic context out of which liberation theology has come, and material on the role of the United States in Central America, the following are helpful:

Raymond Bonner, *Weakness and Deceit: U.S. Policy and El Salvador* (New York: Times Books, 1984)

Roy Gutman, *Banana Diplomacy: The Making of American Policy in Nicaragua, 1981–1987* (New York: Simon & Schuster, 1988)

Walter LaFeber, *Inevitable Revolutions: The United States in Central America,* expanded ed. (New York: W. W. Norton & Co., 1988)

For the benefit of readers who find it hard to relate liberation theology to their own theological understanding, the following table encapsulates some of the differences (reproduced from my *Gustavo Gutiérrez*, p. 91).

Dominant Theology	Liberation Theology
1. responds to the *nonbeliever* whose faith is threatened by modernity	1. responds to the *nonperson* whose faith is threatened by forces of destruction
2. begins with the world of modernity and remains thought-oriented	2. begins with the world of oppression and becomes action-oriented
3. is developed "from above"—from the position of the privileged, the affluent, the bourgeois	3. is developed "from below"—from the "underside of history," the position of the oppressed, the marginated, the exploited
4. largely written by "those with white hands," the "winners"	4. only beginning to be written, must be articulated by those with dark-skinned, gnarled hands, the "losers"
5. focuses attention on a "religious" world that needs to be reinforced	5. focuses attention on a political world that needs to be replaced
6. linked to Western culture, the white race, the male sex, the bourgeois class	6. linked to "the wretched of the earth," the marginated races, despised cultures and sex, the exploited classes
7. affirms the achievements of culture—individualism, rationalism, capitalism, the bourgeois spirit	7. insists that the "achievements" of culture have been used to exploit the poor

8. wants to work gradually, reforming existing structures by "superversion"	8. demands to work rapidly through liberation from existing structures by "subversion"

Chapter Four: A New Way of Being the Church

1. The chapter title comes from Guillermo Cook, *The Expectation of the Poor* (Maryknoll, N.Y.: Orbis Books, 1985), and is also used in Arthur McGovern, *Liberation Theology and Its Critics* (Maryknoll, N.Y.: Orbis Books, 1990).

2. The fullest resource for learning of the history of the church is Enrique Dussel, *A History of the Church in Latin America: Colonialism to Liberation (1492–1979)*, translated and revised by Alan Neely (Grand Rapids: Eerdmans, 1981).

3. The documents for the Medellín and Puebla conferences are available in CELAM, *The Church in the Present-Day Transformation of Latin America in the Light of the Council, II, Conclusions*, CELAM, Bogota, 1970, and in John Eagleson and Philip Scharper, eds., *Puebla and Beyond* (Maryknoll, N.Y.: Orbis Books, 1979).

4. Treatment of the characteristics of the base communities in this section is drawn from Cook, *Expectation of the Poor*, p. 131.

5. The material on the Bible in the base communities is drawn from Gustavo Gutiérrez, *The God of Life* (Maryknoll, N.Y.: Orbis Books, 1991). The quoted matter in this paragraph may be found on p. xvi of that book.

6. The episode about Bishop Casaldáliga is in Carlos Mesters, *Defenseless Flowers* (Maryknoll, N.Y.: Orbis Books, 1990), pp. 3–4.

7. Mesters, *Defenseless Flowers*, p. 2.

8. The following treatment of the "temple" is in Gutiérrez, *Theology of Liberation*, pp. 106–110.

9. The church's response to certain exponents of the base communities is detailed in Harvey Cox, *The Silencing of Leonardo Boff* (Oak Park, Ill.: Meyer-Stone Books, 1988).

10. On the use of the Bible in the base communities and its contribution to their life, the following are especially helpful:

Gustavo Gutiérrez, *The God of Life* (Maryknoll, N.Y.: Orbis Books, 1991)

R. S. Sugirtharajah, ed., *Voices from the Margin: Interpreting the Bible in the Third World* (Maryknoll, N.Y.: Orbis Books, 1991)

Christopher Rowland and Mark Corner, *Liberating Exegesis: The Challenge of Liberation Theology in Biblical Studies* (Louisville, Ky.: Westminster/John Knox Press, 1988)

Ched Myers, *Binding the Strong Man: A Political Reading of Mark's Story of Jesus* (Maryknoll, N.Y.: Orbis Books, 1988)

I am indebted to my pastor, the Rev. Diana Gibson, for the closing quotation from Archbishop Romero.

Chapter Five: Can There Be a New Way for Us? (1)

1. The picture on the front cover is from Philip Scharper and Sally Scharper, eds., *The Gospel in Art by the Peasants of Solentiname* (Maryknoll, N.Y.: Orbis Books, 1984). It, and other paintings in the volume cited, are the work of members of a small fishing community in Nicaragua that was destroyed by Somoza's forces. Each Sunday at mass the group would listen to and reflect upon the

gospel reading for the day. Their comments were and are available in four volumes of *The Gospel in name* (Maryknoll, N.Y.: Orbis Books, 1978–1982). Some of them paint scenes from the gospel story, situated in Nicaraguan cities or countrysides.

2. The letter to Cardinal Gibbons is by Bishop Simeón Pereira y Castelleón and is included in Joseph E. Mulligan, *The Nicaraguan Church and the Revolution*, (Kansas City, Mo.: Sheed & Ward, 1991), p. 67. The book is a particularly useful account of the whole story of church and state in Nicaragua.

3. From *Kairos Central America*, paragraph 90. This document can be found in my edited volume, *Kairos: Three Prophetic Challenges to the Church* (Grand Rapids: Eerdmans, 1990).

4. Material about *kairos* and the *kairos* documents is easily available in the volume cited immediately above, which contains the full text of the three documents, interpretative and historical comments, and reflections on the possible nature of a U.S. document. I have summarized the documents in my *Gustavo Gutiérrez*, pp. 166–178.

By far the best treatment of the ongoing power of idolatry today is Richard Shaull, *Naming the Idols: Biblical Alternatives for U.S. Foreign Policy* (Ocean City, Md.: Skipjack Press, 1992).

The terms *first world, second world,* and *third world* grew out of an international conference at Bandung in 1955, the terms referring, respectively, to the United States, the Soviet Union, and nations (chiefly poor nations from the southern hemisphere) who wanted to avoid alignment with either of the other two. Use of the term is contested by many, who feel that it is demeaning (third world equals third rate?), misleading (in terms of population the third world is actually the "two-thirds world"), and obsolete (the second world having virtually disappeared as a significant world power). Until a better descriptive term emerges, however, the phrase "third world" will continue to be used, standing for the great majority of the human family beset by poverty and lack of independent political power.

Examples of indigenous liberation theologies can be found in Susan Thistlethwaite and Mary Engel, eds., *Lift Every Voice: Constructing Christian Theologies from the Underside* (San Francisco: Harper & Row, 1990), a symposium developing a new theological perspective from the vantage point of the oppressed. Each chapter has suggestions for further reading.

5. This quotation and the one immediately preceding it are from *Kairos Central America,* paragraphs 85–86 (p. 96 in my *Kairos: Three Prophetic Challenges*).

6. *The Road to Damascus,* paragraph 43 (p. 124 in *Kairos: Three Prophetic Challenges*).

7. *Kairos Central America,* paragraph 124 (p. 104 in *Kairos: Three Prophetic Challenges*).

8. *The Road to Damascus,* Conclusion (p. 138 in *Kairos: Three Prophetic Challenges*).

Chapter Six: Can There Be a New Way for Us? (2)

1. The quotation from Wendell Berry's "Manifesto: The Mad Farmer Liberation Front" is found in Wendell Berry, *The Country of Marriage* (New York: Harcourt Brace

Jovanovich, 1973). I am indebted to Diane and John McEntyre for this reference.

2. The distinction between anger and hatred is found in many of the writings of Elie Wiesel. I have developed the distinction more fully in *Elie Wiesel: Messenger to All Humanity*, rev. ed., (Notre Dame, Ind.: University of Notre Dame Press, 1989), pp. 200–203.

3. On the distinctions and similarities between oppressor and oppressed, see Karen Lebacqz, *Justice in an Unjust World* (Minneapolis: Augsburg, 1987), esp. ch. 1.

4. This chapter, and much of the earlier part of the book, has been stimulated by Jack Nelson-Pallmeyer's writings, in particular his most recent book, *Brave New World Order* (Maryknoll, N.Y.: Orbis Books, 1992). His earlier works are still important: *Hunger for Justice, The Politics of Compassion,* and *War Against the Poor,* all published by Orbis Books. In the present chapter, his three proposals are from *Brave New World Order*, ch. 9, pp. 146–155. The direct quotation is from p. 147.

Some of the material in this chapter is treated in greater detail in my "Reflections of a North American: The Future of Liberation Theology," in *Expanding the View: Gustavo Gutiérrez and the Future of Liberation Theology,* ed. Mark Ellis and Otto Maduro (Maryknoll, N.Y.: Orbis Books, 1990), pp. 194–206.